The Theology Handbook

THE DAILY GRACE CO.

Table of Contents

INTRODUCTION — 5

What is Theology? — 5
Why is Theology Important? — 6
Types of Theology — 10
Systematic Theology — 13
   Primary, Secondary, and Tertiary Issues — 14
Branches of Systematic Theology — 17

THEOLOGY PROPER — 19

General Revelation — 20
Special Revelation — 21
The Trinity — 22
Perichoresis — 22
Attributes of God — 24
   Eternal — 26
   Faithful — 28
   Glorious — 31
   Good — 32
   Graciuos — 35
   Holy — 36
   Immutable — 39
   Jealous — 41
   Just — 42
   Love — 45
   Merciful — 46
   Omnipotent — 49
   Omnipresent — 50
   Omniscient — 53
   Wise — 54
   True — 57
   Patient — 58
   Righteous — 61
   Sovereign — 62
   Incomprehensible — 65
   Transcendent — 66
   Immanent — 67
Angel of the Lord — 71
Theophany — 72
Providence — 75

BIBLIOLOGY — 77

Inspiration of Scripture — 79
Inerrancy of Scripture — 82
Sufficiency of Scripture — 85
Eternality of Scripture — 86
Canon — 89
Original Languages of Scripture — 92
Bible Translations — 95

ANTHROPOLOGY — 97

Image of God — 98
Creation Mandate — 101
What is Sin? — 102
The Fall — 105
Original Sin — 106
Condemnation — 109
Total Depravity — 110

CHRISTOLOGY — 113

Incarnation	115
The Deity of Christ	117
The Humanity of Christ	118
Hypostatic Union	119
Offices of Christ	123
The Virgin Birth	126
The Crucifixion	127
The Resurrection	128
The Ascension	129
The Eternal Humanity of Christ	133

SOTERIOLOGY — 135

Overview of How to be Saved	136
Ordo Salutis	138
Election	139
Calling	140
Regeneration	141
Conversion	142
Justification	143
Adoption	145
Sanctification	146
Perseverance	148
Glorification	149
Union with Christ	151
Substitutionary Atonement	152
Double Imputation	155

PNEUMATOLOGY — 157

Personhood of the Holy Spirit	158
Indwelling of the Holy Spirit	159
Fruit of the Spirit	163
Spiritual Gifts	164

ECCLESIOLOGY — 169

The Universal Church, Regional Church, and Local Church	170
Visible and Invisible Church	173
Ordinances and Sacraments	174
Baptism	174
Communion	177
Liturgy	181
Church Government	182

ANGELOLOGY — 187

Angels	188
Demons	191

ESCHATOLOGY — 193

Final Judgment	195
New Heaven and New Earth	196
Resurrection from the Dead	199
Heaven	200
Hell	201
Four Millennial Views	202

APPENDIX

Charts and Illustrations	207

WHAT IS THEOLOGY?

Theology is what we believe about God and how He relates to the universe He created. The word "theology" comes from the Greek words *theos*, which means "God," and *logos*, which means "word" or "reason." A word ending in "-ology" denotes the study of something. Just as biology is the study of life, or anthropology is the study of humans, theology is the study of God. However, the term "theology" encompasses more than characteristics of God Himself. Theology explores what is true about God and what He says is true about the world, humanity, and history. A wide range of topics falls under the category of theology, including the character of God, nature of humans, creation of the universe, constituents of good and evil, and the afterlife.

Everyone has a theology, whether we recognize it or not. We all hold beliefs about God and the universe He created, and what we believe about God influences everything we do. Theology changes the way we treat every person made in His image and profoundly impacts how we live when faced with tragedy and suffering. It transforms the way we approach mundane and monumental moments. Our theology drives everything that we do, and so we must have good, sound theology. Good theology is a theology that aligns with the Word of God, and if we do not actively look to Scripture to form our theology, the world and our sinful nature will form it for us. Theology is not just for pastors or seminary students but for all believers. So let's be good theologians.

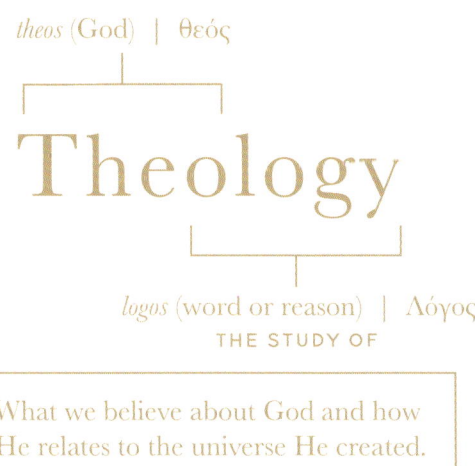

WHY IS THEOLOGY IMPORTANT?

Our theology lays the foundation for how we worship God and love others. In the greatest commandment, Jesus told His followers, "'Love the Lord your God with all your heart, with all your soul, with all your strength, and with all your mind,' and 'your neighbor as yourself'" (Luke 10:27). His directive to love God and neighbor illustrates the importance and necessity of good theology. For how can we love God if we do not know who He? And how do we know what it looks like to love our neighbors as ourselves without any direction? We learn about both of these by studying Scripture. The Bible describes God's character, commands, and deeds and how to love our neighbor well.

Furthermore, our theology informs two important aspects of our faith. First, our theology informs our worship of God. As A.W. Tozer explains in *The Knowledge of the Holy*, "What comes into our minds when we think about God is the most important thing about us. ...Worship is pure or base as the worshiper entertains high or low thoughts of God." If we have poor theology, it will lead us to wrong thoughts of God and false worship of Him. We may view God as a taskmaster who is impossible to please or a kind fatherly figure, never disciplining but freely passing out gifts to all of His children. In either scenario, we misunderstand God's perfect justice and love, which will lead to low-minded worship. Conversely, as we come to a greater knowledge of God, we enjoy His awe-inspiring, holy, and all-satisfying nature through worship.

Second, our theology impacts the way that we tangibly love others. As we meditate on God's character, we learn to love our neighbors as Christ loved us. We discover how to put others above ourselves and love those around us sacrificially. We offer dignity and respect to those unlike us, for they too were made in God's image. As believers, God teaches us to love others by making disciples "of all nations," teaching them to observe all that Jesus commanded them (Matthew 28:18-20). Poor theology might lead us toward an inward preoccupation, too busy to make disciples as we focus our lives on our purposes rather than the Lord's. Or we will inadvertently influence those around us toward a faulty understanding of God, which will lead them to discontentment, idolatry, and sin. Our theology impacts how we love others as we either point them toward the all-sufficiency of Christ or away from it. To biblically love and disciple those around us, we must understand who God is and what He has done for us.

Theology is not for divisive debates or to "puff up" with conceit (1 Corinthians 8:1). Instead, its purpose is to bring worship to our Creator as we love Him in word and truth and as we love those around us in a way that pleases Him.

INTRODUCTION *Why is Theology Important?*

THE IMPACTS OF THEOLOGY

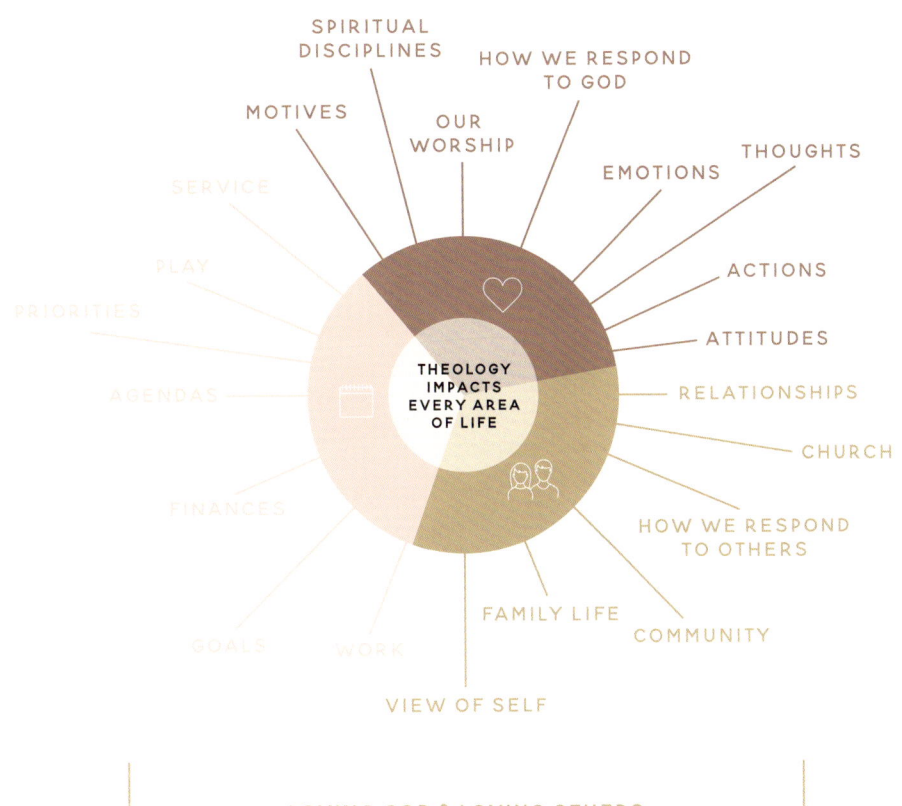

TYPES OF THEOLOGY

Systematic Theology

ORGANIZES THE STUDY OF CHRISTIAN BELIEFS INTO CATEGORIES.

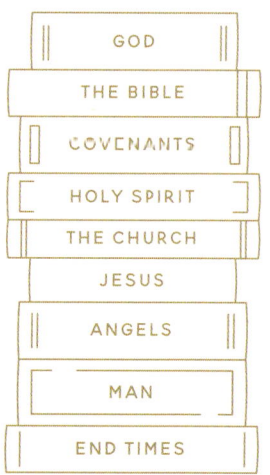

Biblical Theology

TRACES THE DEVELOPMENT OF SCRIPTURAL THEMES AS THEY UNFOLD THROUGHOUT HISTORY.

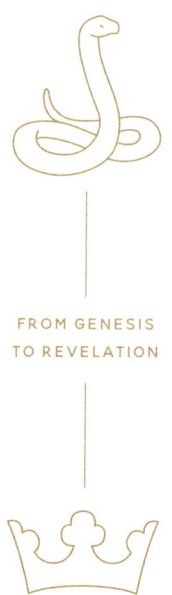

FROM GENESIS TO REVELATION

INTRODUCTION *Types of Theology*

Historical Theology

STUDIES HOW CHRISTIAN BELIEFS HAVE DEVELOPED, CHANGED, OR REMAINED CONSISTENT.

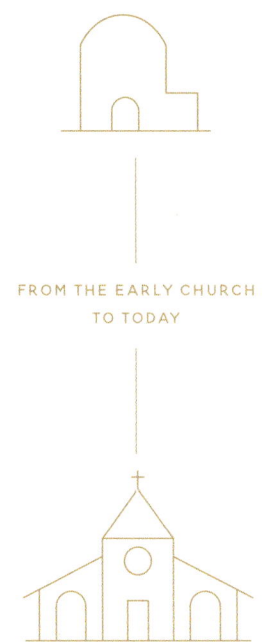

FROM THE EARLY CHURCH TO TODAY

Practical Theology

AIMS TO SHAPE THE BELIEVER'S WORLDVIEW AND LIFE TO BE MORE IN LINE WITH THE WORD OF GOD.

APPLYING THEOLOGY TO

YOURSELF

YOUR CHURCH

THE WORLD

TYPES OF THEOLOGY

While all theology focuses on God and how He relates to the universe He created, there are several different approaches to organizing and studying theological concepts. None of these approaches are "right" or "wrong," rather, each one has a unique focus. Below is a brief overview of four types of theology. While it is important to study all types, this book primarily covers systematic theology and incorporates elements of practical theology to help you apply Scriptural truths to your life.

INTRODUCTION *Types of Theology*

1 SYSTEMATIC

Systematic theology is the categorized study of the beliefs of the Christian faith. This type of theology orders the study of God and everything He has revealed to us through His Word by specific topics such as the study of salvation, Christ, and the end times.

2 BIBLICAL

Biblical theology traces the development of Scriptural themes as they unfold throughout history in God's story of redemption, from Genesis to Revelation. This theology recognizes that Jesus Christ is the center of the Bible and seeks to show how all Scripture points to Him. It examines each biblical book to understand its message, context, and meaning in light of the grand story of redemption. Examples of biblical theology themes are atonement, the temple, marriage, and the kingdom of God.

3 HISTORICAL

Historical theology studies how Christian beliefs have developed, changed, or remained consistent from the formation of the early Church to the Church today. This theology is not a study of Church history, which looks at the history of the Church in the context of the history of the world. Rather, historical theology focuses on the history of what Christians believe.

4 PRACTICAL

Practical theology is when believers take what they have studied in systematic, biblical, or historical theology and ask how it applies to themselves, the Church, and the world around them. Practical theology aims to shape the believer's worldview and life to be more in line with the Word of God.

WE USE *systematic theology* TO HELP US ANSWER THE QUESTION, *"What does the Bible say about this?"* IN A WAY THAT REFLECTS THE WHOLE OF SCRIPTURE.

SYSTEMATIC THEOLOGY

Imagine you are taking a trip to the library. You walk through the doors and are surrounded by shelves upon shelves of books. If you have your heart set on learning about a particular topic, you likely do not begin searching on a random shelf in hopes of finding a book with that topic. Instead, you head toward the categorized section that contains the books about the topic you are searching for.

Systematic theology is like going to the reference section of a library. The reference section is a collection of books providing a brief and concise overview of a particular topic. Likewise, systematic theology takes the doctrines of the Christian faith and organizes them categorically. This theology groups together particular doctrines of Scripture and provides detailed information explaining topics as fully as possible. Just as we look to a reference section to answer questions that we have on a specific subject, we use systematic theology to help us answer the question, "What does the Bible say about this?" in a way that reflects the whole of Scripture.

While the Word of God addresses various topics, its discussion of subjects is often spread throughout the Bible. Systematic theology systematizes the Bible's discussion of multiple topics into categories and distills the information into concrete doctrines. Systematic theology that is faithful to biblical text can help provide trustworthy answers to the questions we may have about important teaching from Scripture. While the Bible is our ultimate authority, systematic theology is devoted to its authority by explaining the truths from Scripture so that we can faithfully live out the Christian life.

Primary, Secondary, and Tertiary Issues of the Christian Faith

As we study theology, it is important to recognize that while some theological teachings, or doctrines, are consistent across all orthodox Christianity, there are many issues where Bible-believing Christians disagree. Though there is one Church made up of all believers around the world, there are many Christian denominations with statements of faith that vary from one another due to doctrinal distinctions. Some are significant distinctions, and others are not. For this reason, it is helpful to have a framework for evaluating the type of importance of various Christian doctrines. The purpose of building a framework is to help believers confidently affirm the gospel of Jesus Christ, appropriately engage in their local churches, and graciously extend respect for debatable issues. The framework submits to the ultimate authority of the Bible; however, it recognizes that not all doctrines are of equal importance.

PRIMARY ISSUES

The primary issues of the Christian faith are doctrines that are essential to the gospel of Jesus Christ. These doctrines are what the Apostle Paul deemed "as most important" (1 Corinthians 15:3-4). They are essential for salvation, and they are rooted in Scripture. Doctrinal issues that fall in this category include the Trinity, the deity of Jesus, the incarnation, the resurrection, salvation by grace alone through faith alone in Christ alone, etc.

SECONDARY ISSUES

Secondary issues refer to doctrines that are non-essential to the gospel but account for the existence of varying denominations. They are nuanced doctrines. While non-fundamental, they are important because they impact the lives of local churches as they shape how churches live out various biblical principles and convictions. These issues are not to be regarded as primary issues affecting the unity of the Church at large. Doctrinal issues that could fall in this category include baptism (infant vs. immersion), the role of women in the church, the present use of spiritual gifts, etc.

INTRODUCTION *Systematic Theology*

TERTIARY ISSUES AND BEYOND

Tertiary issues are doctrines that are non-fundamental to salvation and less immediately urgent. Differences of conviction on these issues typically exist within a denomination. This means that members within a local church can debate these issues and still be within the framework of their denomination's doctrine, even if their different convictions remain. An example of this could be the multiple views regarding the millennium in Revelation. Furthermore, numerous issues are left to personal conscience—matters that are neither explicitly commanded nor forbidden in Scripture. For these issues, each individual should act in alignment with his or her conscience as it is shaped by the principles in God's Word (Romans 14).

APPLICATION

Having a framework for various doctrines of the Christian faith is incredibly necessary for this day and age. As disciples of Jesus, we have a mission to proclaim the gospel (Matthew 28:16-20). To do this effectively, we need to clearly understand the doctrines essential to the gospel (primary issues). The gospel alone is worth our lives. While other issues are still important, we do not need to become hung up on the lesser order issues. This framework guides us in how we should minister to unbelievers. It also impacts how we engage fellow believers, protecting us from unnecessary division.

PRIMARY ISSUES	SECONDARY ISSUES	TERTIARY ISSUES
✓ *Essential doctrines for salvation*	✓ *Non-essential doctrines to the gospel*	✓ *Non-essential doctrines to the gospel*
✓ *Clear in Scripture*	✓ *Shape how churches live out biblical principles/convictions*	✓ *Differences may exist within the framework of a local church's doctrine*
✓ *Examples: the Trinity, deity of Jesus, the incarnation, the resurrection, salvation by grace alone through faith alone*	✓ *Examples: Methods of baptism, role of women in the church, use of spiritual gifts*	✓ *Examples: Millennial views, issues of personal conscience*

BRANCHES OF SYSTEMATIC THEOLOGY

THEOLOGY PROPER

The study of God, His character, and His works

BIBLIOLOGY

The study of the Bible

ANTHROPOLOGY

The study of man

CHRISTOLOGY

The study of Jesus Christ

SOTERIOLOGY

The study of Salvation

PNEUMATOLOGY

The study of the Holy Spirit

ECCLESIOLOGY

The study of the Church

ANGELOLOGY

The study of angels and demons

ESCHATOLOGY

The study of the end times

> IN THIS SECTION

General and Special Revelation

The Trinity

Perichoresis

Attributes of God:

Eternal	*Omnipotent*
Faithful	*Omnipresent*
Glorious	*Omniscient*
Good	*Wise*
Gracious	*True*
Holy	*Patient*
Immutable	*Righteous*
Jealous	*Sovereign*
Just	*Incomprehensible*
Love	*Transcendent*
Merciful	*Immanent*

Angel of the Lord

Theophany

Providence

I

Theology Proper

THE STUDY OF GOD, HIS CHARACTER, AND HIS WORKS

QUESTIONS ANSWERED

Who is God? | *What is God like?* | *What does God do?*

GENERAL REVELATION

God graciously chooses to show us who He is. The ways through which God reveals Himself fall under one of two categories: general revelation or special revelation. General revelation is God's revealing of His nature and character through His creation. Romans 1:20 says, "For His invisible attributes, that is, His eternal power and divine nature, have been clearly seen since the creation of the world, being understood through what He has made." This is the essence of general revelation. God shows the world who He is through His works of creation. The psalmist declares in Psalm 19:1-2, "The heavens declare the glory of God, and the expanse proclaims the work of his hands. Day after day they pour out speech; night after night they communicate knowledge." Nature continually points to the existence and glory of God. Image-bearers of Christ witness His majesty everywhere, from majestic mountains to fields of wildflowers to vast oceans teeming with diverse wildlife and brilliant colors. God's glory is undeniable, and so Scripture rightly says, "It is the fool who says in his heart, 'There's no God'" (Psalm 14:1). No one is excluded from general revelation. Because God has made His existence and power known to all of mankind through His Word and design of the inner man, everyone on earth is held accountable for how they respond and relate to God.

APPLICATION

God has designed the universe and everything in it to undeniably point to His existence and power. He has even graciously placed eternity in the hearts of all mankind (Ecclesiastes 3:11). He has given His image-bearers the gift of human conscience, and it is this conscience that acknowledges the general awareness of God's moral law (Romans 2:14-15). This means that all of mankind knows to a sufficient degree that they fall short of God's holy requirement. The question is, how will each of us respond? The stakes are high. All of us must one day respond individually to who God is and who we are in relation to Him. Every person will be held accountable to His holy standard. Ultimately, while there will be people who willfully reject this knowledge, God is just in upholding His holy standard.

GOD IS REVEALED THROUGH:

SPECIAL REVELATION

While general revelation is God's revealing of Himself through creation, special revelation is God's self-revelation through His Word. The entire Bible is part of God's special revelation, and it is through the study of Scripture that we learn who He is. Occasionally in the Bible, God revealed Himself by appearing to someone directly, which is called a theophany. One example of such an appearance is when the Lord came to Moses in a burning bush. God also spoke to people like Jacob through dreams in the Old Testament. Sometimes He used angels to share His message, and other times God revealed His character through miracles. God has revealed Himself in many ways, but the supreme, special revelation was given to us in Christ when the Word was made flesh to dwell among us. In Hebrews 1:1-2, the writer explains, "Long ago God spoke to our ancestors by the prophets at different times and in different ways. In these last days, he has spoken to us by his Son." God first spoke through the ancestors and prophets in the Old Testament, but He revealed even more of Himself by sending Jesus Christ, who is "the radiance of God's glory and the exact expression of his nature" (Hebrews 1:3).

APPLICATION

Although we can learn about God through His creation, we need the special revelation of His Word to be saved. When we seek to share the love of Christ with our unbelieving family, friends, or neighbors, it is not enough to live in a way that points to the gospel. We must also speak the words of the gospel. God's choice to specially reveal Himself through His Word should compel us to come to Scripture regularly so that we may know Him and love Him more fully. When we approach the Word of God, we should seek to discover first and foremost what it reveals about God's character before asking what it reveals about ourselves or what we should do.

GOD IS REVEALED THROUGH:

THE TRINITY

The word "Trinity" means "three in one," and it describes the nature of God. This doctrine is a primary doctrine of the Christian faith. God is three persons, the Father, the Son, and the Holy Spirit, perfectly united in one essence. The three persons of the Trinity are fully God. They are distinct from one another, exist simultaneously, and are also perfectly united to one another. All three members of the Trinity have existed for all of eternity in perfect love and communion with one another.

APPLICATION

One of the many great comforts of the Trinity is that it assures us that God does not need us. While some say God created humans because He was lonely, the community of the Trinity means that God did not need anyone to fulfill any needs or desires. He was perfectly happy in Himself. This reality means that God did not create us from a place of need but from an overflow of love. And He chose to make us knowing we would rebel against Him. Living with the assumption that God needs us to fulfill His plans, purposes, or desires is a heavy burden to bear, but the Trinity reminds us that He has everything He needs in Himself.

PERICHORESIS

Perichoresis, also known by the Latin-derived term circumincession, is the theological term referring to the mutual indwelling of all three persons of the Trinity. When thinking about the Trinity, we should see all persons of the Trinity as distinct persons who are of one nature. The persons of the Trinity are not separate, independent beings. Rather, they are all one, fully dependent on one another. This mutual indwelling means that the Father is in the Son, the Son is the Father, both are in the Spirit, and the Spirit is in both of them. This term is important because it demonstrates how all members of the Trinity work together. Even though the persons of the Trinity have different roles, they all still work together as one. For example, all persons of the Trinity were involved in the creation, and the salvation of believers comes about by all members of the Trinity working together. Jesus spoke of the unity of the Trinity when He said, "The one who has seen me has seen the Father. How can you say, 'Show us the Father'? Don't you believe that I am in the Father and the Father is in me?" (John 14:9-10). Because all persons of the Trinity mutually indwell together, they are all of the same mind, will, and knowledge.

APPLICATION

Because the three members of the Trinity dwell within each other and are perfectly united, we can trust that they always act consistently with one another. The Father will never contradict the Son, who will never contradict the Spirit. For this reason, we can trust the work and revelation of the members of the Trinity in Scripture, and we can rest in confidence that God does not contradict Himself. He is fully trustworthy.

COMMUNICABLE ATTRIBUTES OF GOD

Attributes that people can reflect

HOLY

LOVE

GOOD

TRUE

JUST

MERCIFUL

GRACIOUS

JEALOUS

PATIENT

WISE

FAITHFUL

THEOLOGY PROPER *Communicable & Incommunicable Attributes of God*

INCOMMUNICABLE ATTRIBUTES OF GOD

Attributes that only God exhibits

ETERNAL

GLORIOUS

IMMUTABLE

OMNIPOTENT

OMNIPRESENT

OMNISCIENT

RIGHTEOUS

SOVEREIGN

ETERNAL

God is eternal, which means He always was, always is, and always will be. God is everlasting, spanning outside time and space. Genesis 1:1 states, "In the beginning, God created the heavens and the earth." This verse suggests that God existed before time began and was present before the creation of the world. God's creative work points to His "eternal power" that has been clearly seen "since the creation of the world" (Romans 1:20). God's eternality is an incommunicable attribute, which means it is a characteristic He alone possesses. We, who are limited and dependent creatures, cannot fully comprehend the grandness of God. Our perception of time is not the same as God's. We have a definitive beginning, and because of sin's effects on our physical condition, we inevitably come to the end of this life in death. Through the prophet Isaiah, God declared that He is the first and the last (Isaiah 44:6). With Moses in Exodus 3:14, God shared His eternal name, I AM. God's eternality described in the Old Testament helps His people recognize the eternal Son who came to save them. The eternal Son, Jesus, declared to be I AM (John 8:58) and "the Alpha and the Omega, the first and the last, the beginning and end" (Revelation 22:13). Jesus was the Word (John 1:1), eternally existing with the Father before the foundation of the world. When Jesus became a man, He stepped into time to defeat sin and death and restore eternality to God's creation.

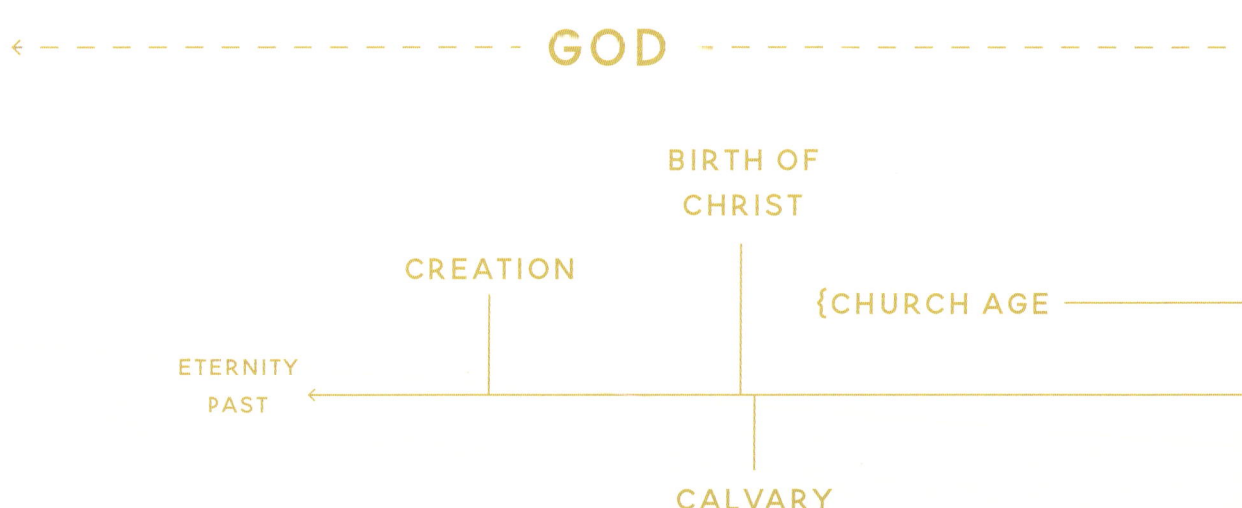

THE ETERNALITY OF GOD

THEOLOGY PROPER *Attributes of God: Eternal*

APPLICATION

We rest in the knowledge that He, who is eternal, meets us in our every moment. He holds each moment in His hands. We are not eternal, but we were made for eternity. We have a definite beginning, and through the power of the gospel, we are given eternal life without end in Christ. Even when we experience death and the end of things in this life, we have hope that we will join the Father who inhabits eternity. This is the power of the resurrected Jesus. He has conquered death for us and gives His children life that will not end. Ecclesiastes 3:11 tells us that God has put eternity in our hearts. He has created us to live for things that last forever. We are tempted to turn to things that are not eternal for satisfaction, affirmation, and fulfillment, but temporal things will never satisfy a heart made to feast on the eternal. The eternal God is the only one who will satisfy the longings of our hearts.

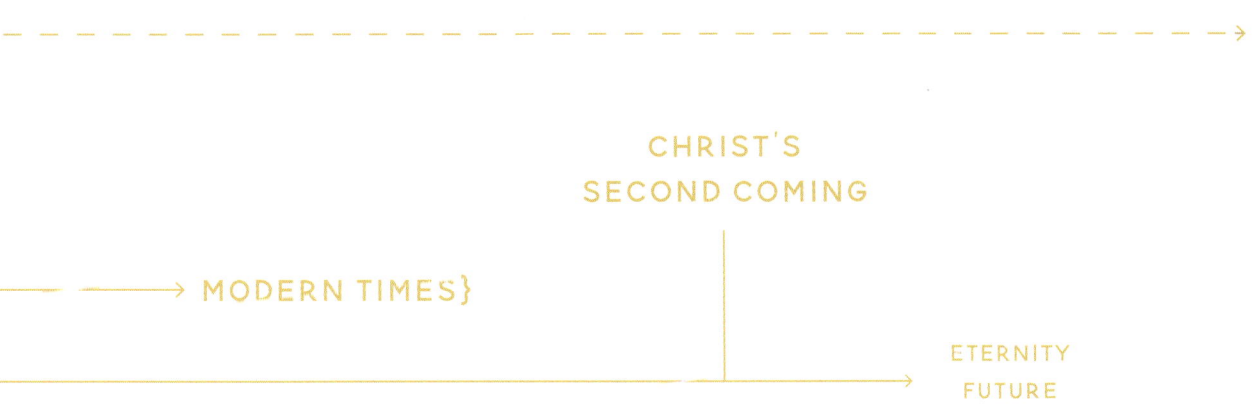

FAITHFUL

God displays His faithfulness in that He always does what He says He will do. The Bible is full of God's covenants, which are binding promises that God makes and keeps. He never forfeits His Word. Whether a promise or a prophecy, He always fulfills His Word because He is faithful. And we give thanks that God's faithfulness is not dependent on anything that we do or do not do; He is faithful because He cannot deny Himself (2 Timothy 2:13). Faithful is who He is, and He is incapable of acting in any way that displays anything other than faithfulness. This means that whatever He has planned, He will always bring to pass. He is loyally devoted to His plan and purpose, which includes the redemption of His people through His Son, Jesus Christ. God's faithfulness is a communicable attribute, which means that we, as His image-bearers, are called to emulate His faithfulness. When we put our faith in Christ, we are given the indwelling Spirit, and He is the One who produces the fruit of faithfulness in our lives (Galatians 5:22). Like God, we are to keep our word. We are to be trustworthy and dependable, but unfortunately, we will not do this perfectly. For, in our sin, we are unfaithful. We are wayward and forgetful creatures; we are covenant-breakers. However, by His grace, we respond to His steadfastness by pursuing faithfulness.

APPLICATION

God's faithfulness means that we can trust Him in every area of our lives. Because His faithfulness depends on His character and not on our actions, we can rest in the knowledge that there is nothing we can do to keep His promises from being fulfilled. We can trust Him, even when we do not understand what He is doing. As we consider His steadfastness throughout redemptive history, our hope in His future faithfulness should be strengthened (Hebrews 10:23). When we face the brokenness of this world, and our hearts grow weary, we can recount His faithfulness and rely on His covenant-keeping nature. Because He is faithful, we can know and trust that He will strengthen those who have placed their faith in Him (1 Corinthians 1:9). Our union with Christ is forever secure because of His faithfulness. We can face our suffering and all else, knowing He will remain faithful to His work of redemption and restoration.

In response to God's faithfulness, we strive to be faithful. This often looks like unseen, ordinary faithfulness in our everyday lives. We remain faithful students of His Word, being hearers and doers (James 1:22). We faithfully proclaim the gospel in word, thought, and deed. We consistently love and serve our neighbors, being trustworthy and dependable as a way to showcase this attribute of God. As we meditate on His love and faithfulness, we echo the psalmist in Psalm 98:4-5 who exclaims, "Let the whole earth shout to the Lord; be jubilant, shout for joy, and sing. Sing to the Lord with the lyre, with the lyre and melodious song." We give thanks to the Lord, call on His name, and tell the world of His wondrous works (Psalm 105:1-2).

THEOLOGY PROPER *Attributes of God: Faithful*

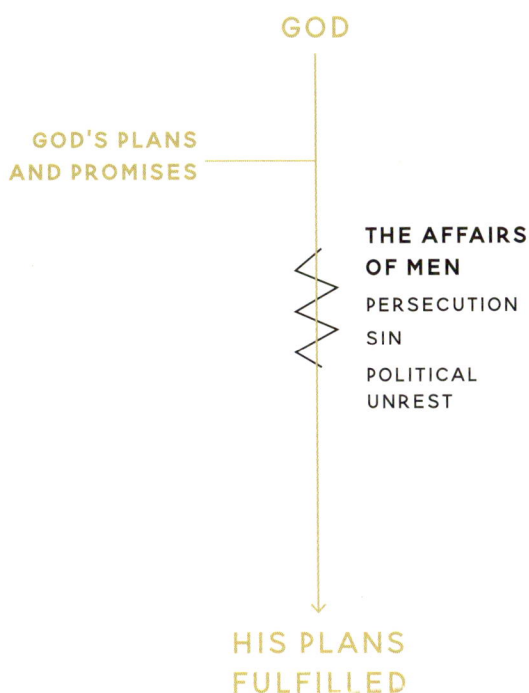

THE FAITHFULNESS OF GOD

GOD

GOD'S PLANS AND PROMISES

THE AFFAIRS OF MEN
PERSECUTION
SIN
POLITICAL UNREST

HIS PLANS FULFILLED

MAN'S HIGHEST CALLING

GLORIOUS

Throughout all of Scripture, we see references to the glory of God. God's glory is a dominant theme in the biblical narrative, and "the glory of God" is a common phrase used by believers. Believers are commanded to do all things to the glory of God (1 Corinthians 10:31). Psalm 19:1 says, "The heavens declare the glory of God." God alone is glorious, and He is zealous for His glory. It is the purpose of everything in heaven and on earth. But what is the glory of God? Throughout Scripture, we see His glory presented as light. He manifests himself as light, and it is through this visible light that His glory is revealed, even if only in part. Our finite minds cannot fully comprehend the fullness of the glory of God. It is an attribute that He alone possesses. It is who He is. It is His intrinsic worth. No one can add to or take away from His glory. It is all of His attributes combined. It is why He alone is worthy of all praise and honor. John 1:14 says, "The Word became flesh and dwelt among us. We observed His glory, the glory as the one and only Son from the Father, full of grace and truth." Jesus Christ, the Son of God incarnate, has revealed the glory of God to us by becoming human and coming to us.

APPLICATION

The highest calling of every man and woman is to glorify God. By His grace, we respond to who He is by worshiping Him. That is what it means to glorify Him! In response to God's intrinsic glory—the greatness of who He is in all of His combined attributes—we are to ascribe or give credit to His glory. Psalm 96:7 says, "Ascribe to the Lord, you families of the peoples, ascribe to the Lord glory and strength." This is the intended purpose of all mankind: to glorify God whose image we bear. We glorify Him by declaring what is true about Him. We also do so by growing in godliness and displaying who He is through the way we live our lives, for it is in doing so that the world can see His worth. And we accomplish these things in partnership with the Spirit as we read and study His Word. The Spirit illuminates the Word and sanctifies us, growing us in Christlikeness. Practically speaking, there are many ways to glorify God. In fact, we are commanded in Scripture to "do everything for the glory of God"—no matter what the "everything" entails for our individual lives (1 Corinthians 10:31). Each of us most effectively glorifies God when we enjoy Him. As believers, may our lifelong goal be to show the world the glory of our great God.

GOOD

God is good, and all that He does is good. The Psalmist affirms this truth in Psalm 119:68 when he exclaims, "You are good, and you do what is good; teach me your statutes." God's goodness means that every part of His character is worthy of approval. He is the standard for what is right, the definition of what is good, and His goodness has no limit. His character is pure, and all that He does is marvelous. Every aspect of His being is perfection, even His justice and wrath. He is sinless and trustworthy, never doing wrong, and He upholds His promises. His goodness is displayed in His creation of the sun and the breathing of life into the tiniest ant. It is shown in His salvation of sinners and the sustaining of His children. God not only creates what is good (Genesis 1), He is also the source of every good thing (James 1:17). And in this goodness, God has revealed Himself to us by sending His Son and giving us His Word.

APPLICATION

God's goodness enables us to trust Him in every season of life. We can trust Him even when we may not understand what He is doing or disagree with His decisions. His goodness empowers us to trust that our limited perspectives cannot possibly understand the complexity of His sovereign choices. Because He is our good Father, King, and Savior, we know He does what is best for us. This divine goodness should lead us to worship God in word and deed. As Christians, we seek to glorify God by living pure lives and seeking the good of those around us, putting the needs of others before ourselves. We bring honor to the Lord when, in faith, we defend the weak, protect the vulnerable, and live lives of integrity. God's goodness leads us to worship, trust, and holiness.

JAMES 1:17

Every good and perfect gift is from above,
coming down from the Father of lights,
who does not change like shifting shadows.

THEOLOGY PROPER *Attributes of God: Good*

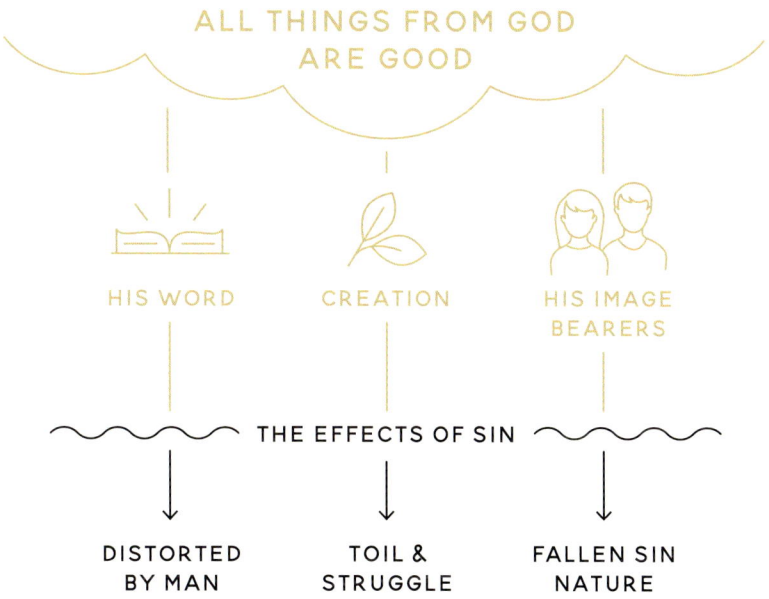

THE GRACE OF GOD
Free & unmerited favor

WHAT WE DESERVE	WHAT GRACE OFFERS
DEATH	ETERNAL LIFE
SEPARATION FROM GOD	COMMUNION WITH GOD
CURSE	BLESSING
JUDGMENT	MERCY
ASHES	BEAUTY

GRACIOUS

Grace is the free and unmerited favor of God. God's grace is a beautiful expression of His steadfast and enduring love that pulls us from the depths of our sin and lavishes us with good gifts that we do not deserve. It may seem surprising that God would show such extravagant grace to people who sin and rebel against their Creator, but from Genesis to Revelation, Scripture displays God's grace again and again. For those who place their faith in Jesus, God's redeeming grace saves them from eternal death, but even unbelievers experience God's common grace. Common grace is grace given to all people, regardless of belief in Him. We see His common grace as He sustains the earth and restrains sin, keeping man's depravity and wickedness from reaching its greatest potential. God's redeeming grace is fully expressed in the gospel. The gospel is the message of God's abounding grace coming to undeserving sinners, not because of their righteousness but because God chose before the foundations of the world to lavish them with His limitless love and overflowing grace. The gospel message is found in the person of Jesus Christ and demonstrated for us on the cross—the cross where He died a death He did not deserve and rose again so that God could fully restore His chosen people to Him.

APPLICATION

God's grace enables us to know and believe in Him. It is how God grants us salvation and makes us new creations in Christ (Ephesians 2:8, 2 Corinthians 5:17). As a new creation, grace also enables us to obey God. When we were dead in our sin, we had no regard for the law and ways of God. Now because of God's grace, we desire to do what God asks of us in His Word (Romans 8:6-11). In His grace, He gives us His Spirit of grace, who empowers us to obey Him. Grace is a communicable attribute of God, so we can reflect God's image and grow in grace as well (2 Peter 3:17-18). We steward this gift and show it to others (1 Peter 4:10). Followers of Jesus should be known for being gracious because they have received abundant, overwhelming, lavish grace. God offered us grace that we did not deserve, and so we are called to be gracious to others who have done nothing to earn it or who have hurt us. When someone harms us or says an unkind word, let our responses be full of mercy. When someone expresses a need, let us be the first to offer help and prayer. As we have been given abundant grace, so we have been called to show this grace to others (Titus 3:1-10).

HOLY

God is holy. To be holy means to be set apart and sacred. It is to be morally blameless, pure, and without sin. The holiness of God makes Him distinct from all of His creation. This attribute also influences all of His other attributes because holiness is who God is. When God acts, speaks, or works in the world, all is done out of His holiness—His utter perfection. God is perfectly free from the power of sin. Everything that God does is right. In 1 Samuel 2:2, Hannah says in her prayer, "There is no one holy like the Lord. There is no one besides you! And there is no rock like our God." The seraphim, which are angelic beings, and other heavenly creatures in the throne room of the Lord call to one another and declare the Lord's holiness saying, "Holy, holy, holy is the Lord of Armies; his glory fills the whole earth" (Isaiah 6:3). That this is the only attribute of God repeated three times in this way indicates this is an essential attribute of God to understand. After the rebellion of man in Genesis 3, the world was filled with sin. Sin is the opposite of holiness as it corrupts and diseases everything in its path. Sin leaves creation the opposite of what God intended it to be. God's holiness drives Him to rid the world of anything that is not holy because it corrupts what He has made. When God saves us through the blood of Jesus, we are restored to a position of holiness in Christ (Hebrews 10:10), and throughout the course of our lives, the Holy Spirit in us sanctifies us, making us more holy as we grow in Christlikeness day by day.

APPLICATION

God's holiness comforts us in every situation, for we know that everything God does is perfect and right. God calls us repeatedly in His Word to be holy as He is holy. We are to flee sin and walk in obedience. All of our words, thoughts, and actions are to be pure. When we see God's complete holiness, we see how severely we fall short, and in turn, we see our desperate need for the Lord. We are incapable of possessing any holiness outside the work of Jesus. But when we are in Christ, the Holy Spirit empowers us to grow in holiness and walk in obedience.

THEOLOGY PROPER *Attributes of God: Holy*

RESPONSE TO GOD'S HOLINESS
Isaiah's vision

SEE GOD'S HOLINESS

SEE OUR SIN

CONFESSION

FORGIVENESS & CLEANSING

COMMISSION

ISAIAH 6:1-9

In the year that King Uzziah died, I saw the Lord seated on a high and lofty throne, and the hem of his robe filled the temple.

Seraphim were standing above him; they each had six wings: with two they covered their faces, with two they covered their feet, and with two they flew.

And one called to another: Holy, holy, holy is the Lord of Armies; his glory fills the whole earth.

The foundations of the doorways shook at the sound of their voices, and the temple was filled with smoke.

Then I said: Woe is me for I am ruined because I am a man of unclean lips and live among a people of unclean lips, and because my eyes have seen the King, the Lord of Armies.

Then one of the seraphim flew to me, and in his hand was a glowing coal that he had taken from the altar with tongs.

He touched my mouth with it and said: Now that this has touched your lips, your iniquity is removed and your sin is atoned for.

Then I heard the voice of the Lord asking: Who will I send? Who will go for us? I said: Here I am. Send me.

IMMUTABLE

God's immutability means that He is unchanging. In Malachi 3:6, God said, "I, the Lord, have not changed," and Hebrews 13:8 says that "Jesus Christ is the same yesterday, today, and forever." Unlike our bodies that grow and age with time, God's nature and essence forever remain the same. His attributes do not increase or diminish. Because God is perfect, if He were to shift in any way, He would cease to be God. His promises and plans never change because His will does not change. He does not change His mind or alter his plans and actions. Whatever He has ordained will come to pass, and what a gift of grace that He allows us to go to Him in prayer as He works through our prayers to bring about His will on the earth. Scripture often compares God's immutability to a rock. Isaiah 26:4 says, "Trust in the Lord forever, because in the Lord, the Lord himself, is an everlasting rock!" As a rock remains firm and unchanging, so does our Heavenly Father, our rock and firm foundation.

APPLICATION

God's immutability means that we can have ultimate security in Him. Like shifting sand, we live in a constantly changing world. Our moods shift, and our bodies age. Our jobs change, and our relationships evolve. Historical events threaten our way of life or sense of safety. Yet, in unpredictable changes, God remains the same. We never need to live in fear that His love for us will change or our position of salvation will shift. Though we may seek security and stability in money, relationships, accomplishments, or other false hopes, those things can change in an instant. The only true and steady anchor for our souls is the steadfast, immovable, unchanging God and His unchanging promises to us.

THE JEALOUSY OF GOD
A good thing

JEALOUS

God is a jealous God, meaning He desires to receive the praise and affection He rightly deserves. He would not be God if He desired glory to go other places because He is the only one worthy of glory in the entire universe. When God desires praise, it is because He wants to magnify the source of all good, holiness, purity, love, righteousness, and justice. He is not jealous in the way that humans are jealous. His jealousy is not selfish or sinful, as is so often the case in the jealousy of humanity. It is not bitter, and it does not harm. Rather, God's jealousy for His glory is a gracious thing, for when we glorify anyone or anything else above Him, we will be unsatisfied and without real hope. His jealousy manifests itself in the salvation of His people and the condemnation of those who are in opposition to Him. Because He is jealous for His glory, He is right and loving to require that His people remain fully devoted to Him. When they misplace their worship and give glory to idols, He calls them back, demanding them to be faithfully devoted to Him.

APPLICATION

The jealousy of God compels us to a life of service to our King. It moves us to live for His glory and not our own. It reminds us of His steadfast love that pursues us when we sin and calls us to repentance and faith. The jealousy of God enables us to live a life free from fear as we rest in God's sovereign pursuit of His glory. The jealousy of God is not something that we should fear or be uncertain of but something in which we should delight.

EXODUS 34:14

Because the Lord is jealous for his reputation,
you are never to bow down to another god.
He is a jealous God.

JUST

God is just, which means He always does what is right. Divine justice is an outworking of God's holiness. Because God is just, He must punish sin. A good judge executes justice. If a judge let the guilty go free and criminals walk away without punishment, we would rebuke that judge as unjust and bad. God is the perfect judge because He will not allow any sin, no matter how great or small, to go unpunished. Sin disrupts the union between God and man and has broken our world, and it is just for God to respond with wrath. God exercises His justice to set things right. 2 Chronicles 19:7 says, "there is no injustice or partiality or taking bribes with the Lord our God." God does not extend favoritism by giving justice to some people and not to others, nor can one bribe Him to refrain from exerting His justice. As a good, fair, and loving judge, God executes His justice perfectly and fairly. God's justice does not oppose His mercy and grace but goes hand in hand with it. God's mercy and justice meet at the cross where Christ bore the sins of God's people and paid the penalty of death in our place. God's wrath in response to sin has been poured out upon Christ on our behalf. Our failure to obey God's law deserves punishment, but Jesus Christ has taken that punishment upon Himself and given us mercy.

APPLICATION

As we look at our world, it is evident that injustice resides in every corner. It can seem that evil runs rampant without punishment. But while injustice occurs and evil-doers may appear to prosper, God's final act of judgment will cause all sin to receive its due punishment. We must not become discouraged by the sin around us but await the day when God will set all things right. As a response to God's justice, we, too, are to be people of justice. We are to treat others fairly and justly, not taking advantage of the forgiveness we have received by mistreating others. We are to fight for the just cause of the oppressed and take a stand against wickedness. We are to act justly, love faithfulness, and walk humbly with our God (Micah 6:8).

MICAH 6:8

Mankind, he has told each of you what is good and what it is the Lord requires of you: to act justly, to love faithfulness, and to walk humbly with your God.

THEOLOGY PROPER *Attributes of God: Just*

Christ bears God's wrath so that we can receive mercy.

LOVE

God's love is inherent to who He is. His love is steadfast, unconditional, perfect, and sufficient. It does not change, and it cannot be altered. It has existed for all time among the members of the Trinity, and God set His love on those He would save before He even created them. God pursues us with a never-ending, abundant, and faithful love. He did not love us because we were worthy of His love. Instead, God demonstrated His love for us by sending His only Son into the world while we were still enemies, bearing our sins and dying the death that we deserved (Romans 5:8). His love is sacrificial, and it upholds His faithful covenant with His people. God pours it out to His children through His Spirit, which lives inside us, and it is expressed through His patience, grace, and mercy toward all. His love is complete; it needs nothing. It is sufficient to satisfy the deepest longings of our hearts.

APPLICATION

God's love for us is unconditional, steadfast, and complete. We cannot earn it by obeying Him, nor can we lose it by living lives of rebellion. Nothing could make God love us any more or less. God's unconditional love frees us from living lives on the figurative treadmill, endlessly trying to do enough good deeds to earn God's favor. We already have His complete favor through Christ. Instead, we are freed to obey Him out of our gratitude. When we know God's love and understand His grace, it changes us. It helps us surrender every idol that hinders us and joyfully run the race that He has marked out for us. We can love God because He first loved us (1 John 4:19).

Furthermore, when we experience God's love, we can share His love with others. God did not love us with a convenient love; rather, while we were still His enemies, He bore our sins on his faultless body and died on the cross, making a way to save us. In the same way, we are now called to emulate this sacrificial love to those around us. When we are in conflict, whether with a friend, enemy, or stranger, we can remember God's all-sufficient love that moves toward the unlovable. When we engage with a person who feels difficult to love, we remember that we, too, were difficult, yet Christ's love endured. As God loved us, so we are to love one another.

MERCIFUL

God is merciful. To extend mercy is to withhold a rightly deserved punishment or judgment against someone. Mercy meets a person's despair with goodness. To say that God is merciful is to say that He is compassionate, patient, caring, forgiving, tender-hearted, selfless, loving, gracious, and kind. The Hebrew word *hesed* is often translated as "mercy." It is a difficult word to translate succinctly, but it refers to God's covenant love, which is unbreakable. God has always been merciful. From the beginning, God planned to send His Son, Jesus Christ, to die for our sins so that we might receive mercy and have life everlasting with Him in heaven.

To offer mercy costs something. God's mercy is His graciousness, goodness, and compassion confronting human depravity, brokenness, and guilt. He does not owe us such mercy but freely gives it (Titus 3:5). This is why the mercy of God is seen most clearly in the person and work of Jesus Christ. He willingly emptied Himself and took on the likeness of humanity to accomplish the Father's plan of redemption (Philippians 2:7). This plan involved the cross, which demonstrates God's mercy. For it was on this cross that Christ drank the cup of God's wrath. Crushed as a guilt offering, He gave His life for the sins of many, satisfying the punishment that our sins so rightly deserved (Isaiah 53:10).

APPLICATION

When we receive God's mercy, we are transformed. We extend mercy to others as a way to showcase the mercy that was freely and sovereignly given to us by God in Christ. In mercy and because of mercy, we can demonstrate love, compassion, forgiveness, and grace to others, putting the riches of God's glory on display. Through His mercy, we are not merciless, nor are we vengeful or hateful toward others. We do not demand perfection but willingly enter into the imperfection and mess of others alongside them. We absorb the cost of offenses and meet the needs of others with goodness, compassion, and forgiveness. We sacrifice our comforts to relieve the tangible and intangible needs of others. We do so wisely, not condoning abuse, to any degree, against ourselves or others. In being merciful, we are happy in the Lord and continue to receive His mercies new every morning (Matthew 5:7, Lamentations 3:22-23).

THEOLOGY PROPER *Attributes of God: Merciful*

THE MERCY OF GOD

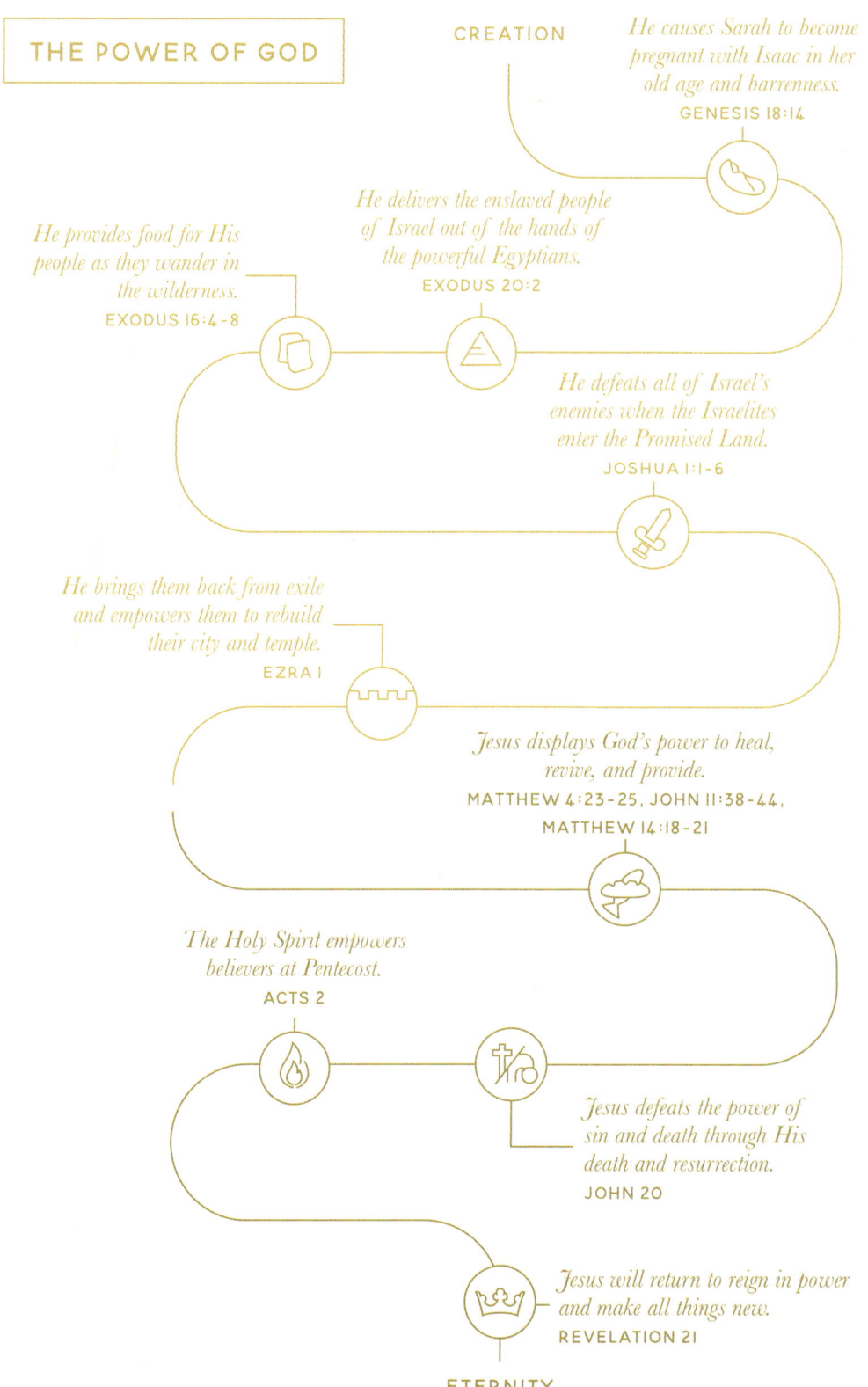

OMNIPOTENT

God is omnipotent, which means He is all-powerful. He holds all power, and His power is limitless. He has created all things, and He sustains all of creation. The Lord's omnipotence also means that He does not grow faint or weary, and He does not need a break to regain strength (Isaiah 40:28). He operates out of complete power at all times. While many people in our world abuse power, using it to serve themselves, God uses His power perfectly and always for our good and His glory.

APPLICATION

If you are a follower of Christ, God's power won salvation for you on your behalf (Ephesians 2:8-9). And the Lord does not leave you on your own after He saves you. The Spirit of God who raised Christ from the dead comes to live inside us. He powerfully works to help us overcome our sin and transforms us to reflect our Father (Romans 8:11). Every event in your life is under the power and authority of your loving, gracious, and wise Heavenly Father. The Lord is intimately involved and in control of the situations and decisions you face. And He works to weave these things together to bring glory to Himself and grow you in sanctification, even when some of these events seem hopeless and bring suffering. God's power works to use everything in our lives for our good.

Even though we foolishly try to gain power through avenues such as money, beauty, and status to esteem ourselves, we will never possess such power as our almighty and powerful God. We are powerless compared to the Lord, which causes us to rely fully on Him and understand that He is the source of any strength we possess. We can find true rest in the knowledge of His omnipotence as we accept our limitations, knowing that when we are weak, then we are strong (2 Corinthians 12:9-10).

2 CORINTHIANS 12:9

But he said to me, "My grace is sufficient for you, for my power is perfected in weakness." Therefore, I will most gladly boast all the more about my weaknesses, so that Christ's power may reside in me.

OMNIPRESENT

God is omnipresent, which means He is present everywhere (Psalm 139:7-10). A physical body does not restrain Him (1 Kings 8:27). God is also fully present in all places. He is not distracted by the events of the world while trying to listen to the prayers of His people. God is everywhere. He knows exactly what is happening in every place and is sovereignly in control of it all. This means that the God who gave His promise to Abraham and his descendants is the same God who dwells inside of us today through the Holy Spirit (2 Corinthians 6:16). And when we pass away, God will still be present and at work in the world. We are limited by space and time, but God is everywhere.

APPLICATION

God's omnipresence means that we are never alone. If you leave home and move to a new state, He is with you. When you are physically alone and frightened, He is there. As church bodies gather across the world, He is present in each one. Though we cannot see Him with us as we see our families and the sun and trees, His presence is greater and richer than the created things of this world because He is their Creator. The Lord's presence with us should be sobering, for there are many things we do in secret in His presence that we would never do in the company of others. The Lord sees and knows everything we do. But as we fight to overcome sin in our lives, the presence of God still comforts us. We can continually rely on Him because He is always there. Even when we feel He is far away, He is not. He is with us always.

PSALM 139:7-10

Where can I go to escape your Spirit? Where can I flee from your presence?
If I go up to heaven, you are there; if I make my bed in Sheol, you are there.
If I fly on the wings of the dawn and settle down on the western horizon,
even there your hand will lead me; your right hand will hold on to me.

THEOLOGY PROPER *Attributes of God: Omnipresent*

GOD'S OMNIPRESENCE

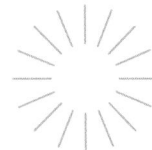
GOD IS NOT RESTRAINED BY A PHYSICAL BODY

GOD IS FULLY PRESENT IN ALL PLACES

GOD HEARS OUR PRAYERS UNDISTRACTED BY WORLD EVENTS

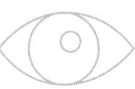
GOD KNOWS WHAT IS HAPPENING AND IS SOVEREIGN OVER ALL

GOD'S MANIFEST PRESENCE

THEOPHANIES

DWELT IN THE TABERNACLE AND TEMPLE

THE INCARNATION OF JESUS CHRIST

GOD IS PRESENT IN EVERY CHURCH BODY AS THEY GATHER AROUND THE WORLD

WALKED WITH MAN IN THE GARDEN OF EDEN

DWELLS WITH US IN THE NEW CREATION

LIMITED KNOWLEDGE:

WE SEE ONLY PIECES OF GOD'S PLAN

INFINITE KNOWLEDGE:

GOD SEES THE WHOLE PICTURE

OMNISCIENT

God is omniscient, which means He is all-knowing. In His omniscience, God knows everything fully—not a single detail escapes His knowledge. Unlike humans who gain knowledge through external means, God does not have to discover information, nor does He lack any information. David writes in Psalm 139:6, "This wondrous knowledge is beyond me. It is lofty; I am unable to reach it." By His perfect nature, He has perfect knowledge. God knows all that has been, all that is now, and all that there will be. While we may experience times when new information alarms us, because of His omniscience, nothing ever surprises God. Since God created the world, He knows everything about it. Nothing that takes place in His creation is a mystery to Him, including us. His omniscience allows Him to know us personally and intimately. He knows every thought, feeling, and word from our mouth, even before we speak it.

APPLICATION

God's omniscience should be a great comfort to believers. David writes in Psalm 131:1-2 in response to God's knowledge, "I do not get involved with things too great or too wondrous for me. Instead, I have calmed and quieted my soul like a weaned child with its mother." Because God knows everything, we do not have to. We can leave matters in His hands, trusting that God knows what is happening even if we do not, and He will handle things rightly. He knows our needs before we even ask them, and we can rest secure that God will never fail to take care of His children. Through His omniscience, there is great freedom for believers. Because of Christ's work on the cross, believers enter into a deeply intimate relationship with God. He may know our iniquities, but we can rest in the grace of Jesus that allows us to be fully known and fully loved despite our sin. We can find freedom in knowing that there is nothing to hide from God. We stand fully exposed to Him in our sin, yet He loves us still the same.

*"God knows all that has been,
all that is now,
and all that there will be."*

WISE

God is perfect in wisdom. Wisdom is not only knowing information about something but understanding the right way to do something. God knows all things, but He also knows what is good—what is best. Because our human perspective is limited, we search for what is wise. And though we may often think we are making the right decisions, those decisions may sometimes prove to be unwise in the end. However, because God knows everything, He always makes wise judgments. In Scripture, wisdom is connected to morality. Proverbs 8:20 says, "I walk in the ways of righteousness, along the paths of justice." God says and executes all things according to His perfect wisdom; He commits no foolish or unrighteous act. 1 Corinthians 1:30 tells us, "It is from him that you are in Christ Jesus, who became wisdom from God for us—our righteousness, sanctification, and redemption." God is the standard for all wisdom, which means that any understanding of wisdom is found only in Him. The gospel itself is described as the wisdom of God. Scripture explains how worldly wisdom results in foolishness and destruction, while the wisdom of God leads to salvation.

APPLICATION

No earthly wisdom compares to the wisdom of God. While people here on earth believe that their knowledge or skills make them wise, we only find true wisdom in knowing God and His Word. Scripture tells us that the fear of the Lord is the beginning of all wisdom (Psalm 111:10). As we grow in our understanding of God and His Word, we grow in wisdom. God's Word reveals how to live a godly life, and as we are obedient to His Word, such obedience produces wisdom as we learn and grow. We do not look to ourselves to make wise decisions but to His Word to make correct judgments. In addition to searching God's Word for the wisdom He offers, we can also come to Him in prayer. James 1:5 says, "Now if any of you lacks wisdom, he should ask God—who gives to all generously and ungrudgingly—and it will be given to him." In our pursuit of wisdom, we can turn to the One who is the very definition of wisdom.

THEOLOGY PROPER *Attributes of God: Wise*

NOW IF ANY OF YOU

lacks wisdom,

HE SHOULD

ask God

— WHO GIVES TO ALL
GENEROUSLY & UNGRUDGINGLY —
AND IT WILL BE

given to him.

JAMES 1:5

REFLECTING GOD'S TRUTHFULNESS

TRUTHFULNESS
- PROCLAIMING GOD'S PROMISES
- STUDYING SCRIPTURE
- HONESTY
- EVANGELISM
- LIVING BY THE WORD
- INTEGRITY

UNTRUTHFULNESS
- HYPOCRISY
- FLATTERY
- DECEITFULNESS
- SEEKING OUR OWN TRUTH
- PROCLAIMING MAN'S WISDOM
- SLANDER

TRUE

God is true, which means that in Him, no falsehood exists. God does not lie because lying is contrary to His nature. Jeremiah 10:10 says that "the Lord is the true God; he is the living God and eternal King." As the one true God, He always projects a genuine reflection of Himself. Every aspect of His character and all that He proclaims about Himself is wholly true in every way. What He says in His Word is as true today as it was when it was written. God never makes a promise He will not fulfill. Because God is true, He is also the standard of truth, and the truth is determined by comparing statements to Christ and His Word.

APPLICATION

Because God is true, we can trust Him. Unlike humans who can put on a facade and are untrustworthy, we can completely trust God's character. God has also shown that He is trustworthy through Scripture. We can read His promises in Scripture and see how He has already fulfilled many promises through Jesus Christ. Therefore, we can trust that any unfulfilled promises will come to pass. Because we know that God is trustworthy, it is vital that we do not seek to find our own truth or follow people who claim to have truth apart from God's Word. We only find truth in God. And His truthfulness compels us to be people of truth—in both what we allow into our minds and what we share with others. By walking in integrity, speaking truthfully, and refraining from deceit, believers reflect the character of God.

> *His truthfulness compels us to be people of truth—in both what we allow into our minds and what we share with others.*

PATIENT

God is patient, long-suffering, and slow to anger (Exodus 34:6-7, Psalm 86:15, Psalm 103:8). His patience is not limited but is abundantly poured out to all of humanity. At the same time, God's patience does not mean that He does not notice sin or that He will not show justice. Numbers 14:18 says, "The Lord is slow to anger and abounding in faithful love, forgiving iniquity and rebellion. But he will not leave the guilty unpunished." God is not rash in displaying anger as He delays punishment by giving those who have sinned time to turn from their evil ways and follow Him (2 Peter 3:9, Romans 2:4). He is long-suffering toward His enemies and provides an opportunity for all to come to repentance (1 Timothy 1:16, Romans 9:22, 1 Peter 3:20). God has expressed His patience toward us through His steadfast love and in Christ, who patiently loved sinners and endured the suffering of the cross for our sins.

APPLICATION

Patience is an expression of the fruit of the Spirit, though one that is often a challenging practice in our lives (Galatians 5:22-23). However, we should be "slow to anger" with the difficult people in our lives, just as He is (Psalm 103:8). When our patience is tested, we can look to Christ, who faithfully endured suffering as well as difficult people. By the Spirit's power, we can begin to grow in love, joy, peace, and patience with others. Practically, this may mean that we do not immediately condemn others for their mistakes but extend to them the benefit of the doubt. When we are wronged, before being quick to demand vengeance, let us remember that vengeance is the Lord's, and He will repay (Romans 12:19). Just as God is patient with us, so we too are called to be patient with one another (Colossians 3:12, James 5:7-8). We can remain patient in trials because we know that the Lord is coming soon (James 5:8). He will one day make all things new and right every wrong. When we experience hardship and desire immediate relief, we remember that God's timing is perfect, and when He returns, He will wipe away every tear from our eyes.

> **HIS PATIENCE IS NOT LIMITED BUT IS ABUNDANTLY POURED OUT TO ALL OF HUMANITY.**

THEOLOGY PROPER *Attributes of God: Patient*

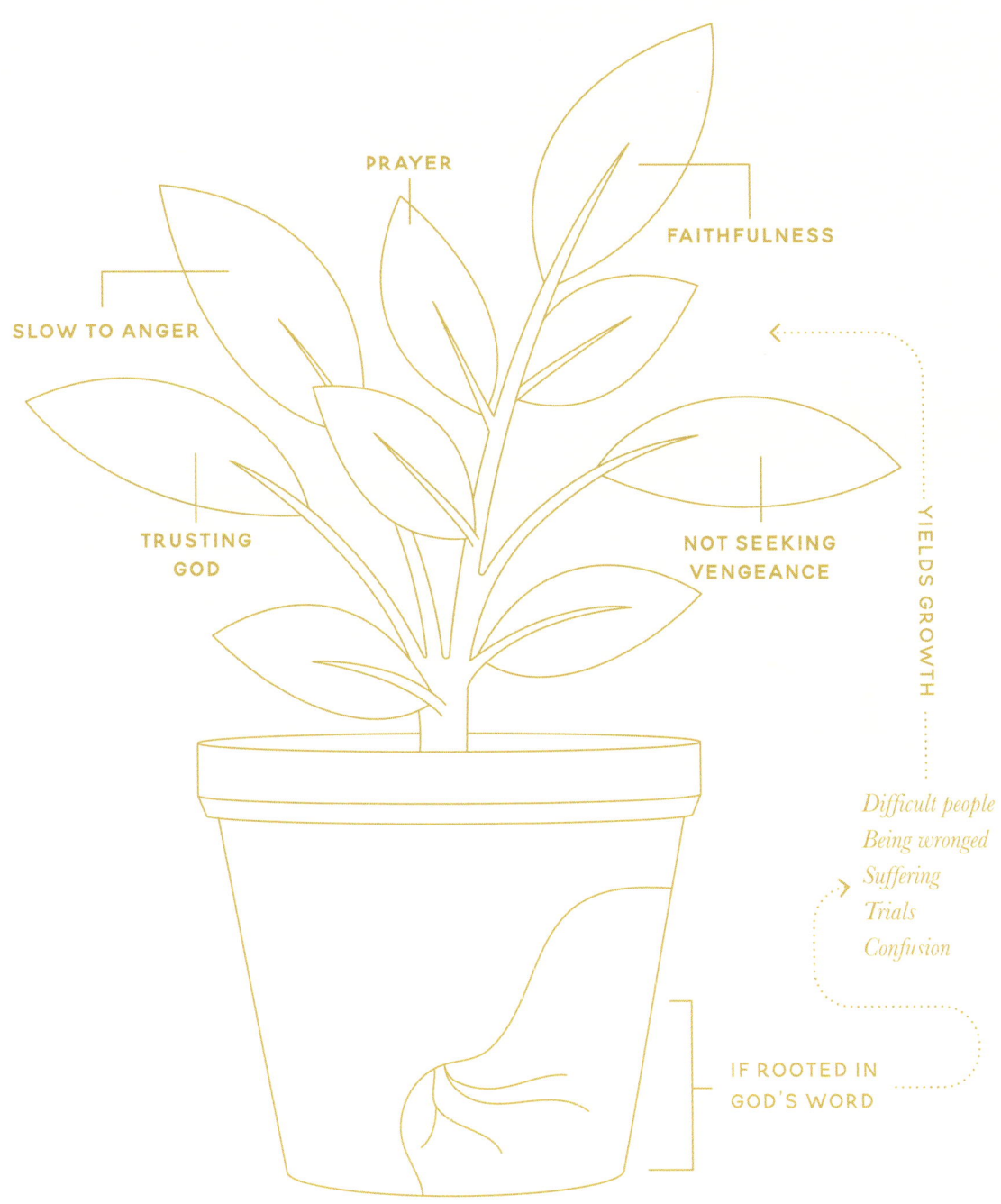

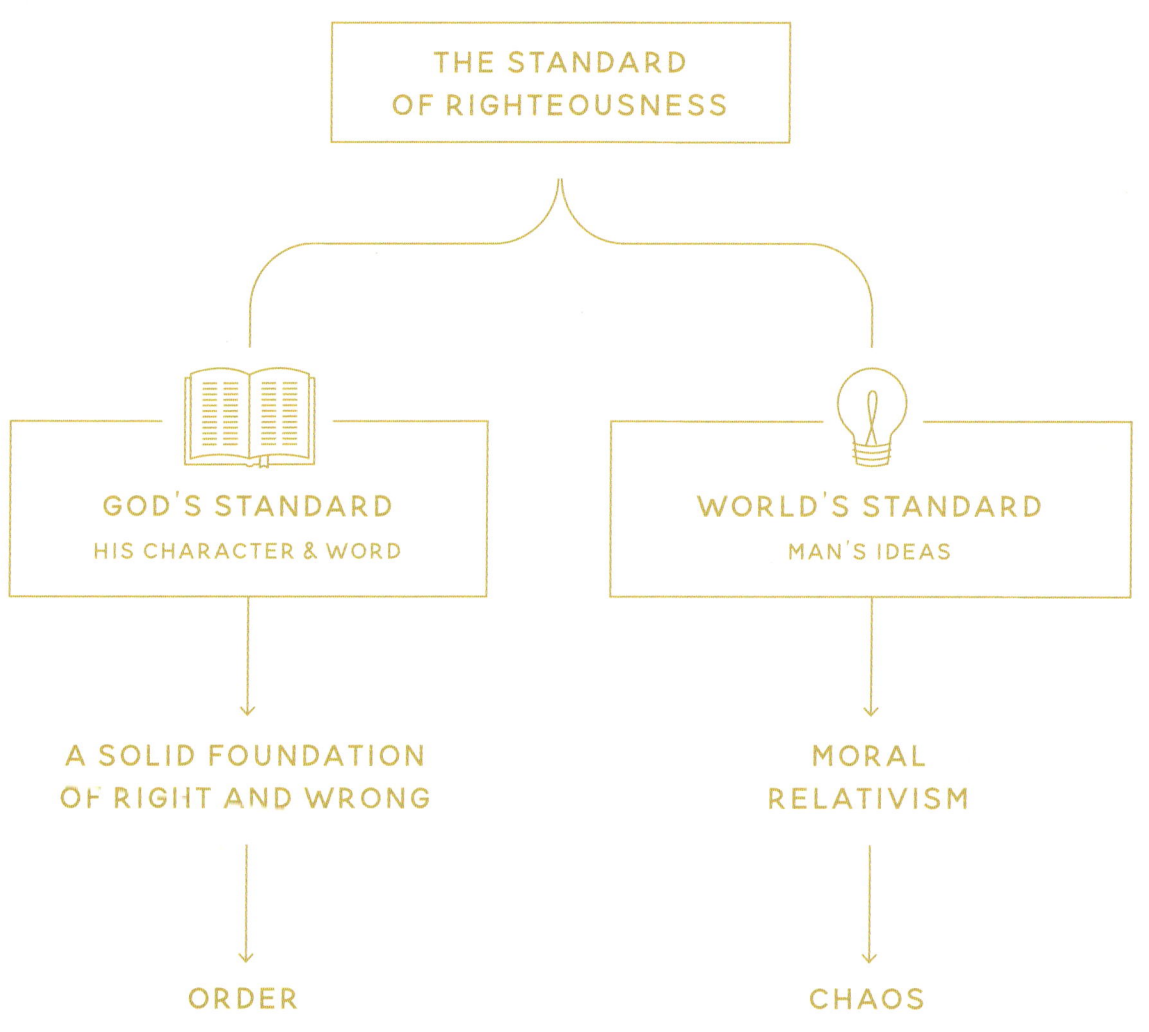

RIGHTEOUS

God is righteous, which means that all of His ways are perfectly moral and just. It is in God's nature to always do what is right. God has set a moral law that is in accordance with His nature. However, this standard of righteousness is not above Him or beyond Him, nor did God create it. Rather, His moral standard is Himself. His ways are righteous because He is righteous. His righteousness is an expression of His holy nature, and just as His nature is perfect, so is His Law. Psalm 19:7-9 says, "the instruction of the Lord is perfect, renewing one's life." God commands only what is morally right, and all of His actions follow the perfect Law He has established. Through the moral law, God calls us to imitate His character. The righteousness expected of us is the same righteousness reflected in God's holy, loving, and just character.

APPLICATION

Our world often struggles to find a standard for what is right and what is wrong, and whether something is morally right is considered to be subjective. However, because God is completely righteous, He is the standard for what is right. We should not follow the world's standard of righteousness but instead look to the character and nature of God to display the righteous, moral law. God has set forth what is right in response to His own righteousness, and the pages of Scripture reveal how to live obediently. Unfortunately, we all fall short of obeying God's moral law, and none of us are righteous. However, through Christ's work on the cross, believers are given His perfect righteousness. We are declared righteous because of His righteousness imputed to us, which means that we are declared holy by God when we put our faith in Jesus. In response, we live righteously by our character and conduct and no longer need to fear God's punishment when we fall short.

HIS WAYS ARE RIGHTEOUS BECAUSE HE IS RIGHTEOUS.

SOVEREIGN

God is sovereign, which means He is totally in control. He has full power and authority over His creation—heaven and earth, everything and everyone. There is nothing that happens apart from His willing it to happen, and likewise, there is nothing that can stop His plans from coming to pass. Nothing is outside of His control, and God sovereignly works in all things for our good and His glory. He has an eternal plan (Ephesians 1:9-11), and that plan includes redeeming His people to Himself through the blood of His Son (1 Peter 1:18-19). Throughout history, God has worked in all things to accomplish His purposes, and He does so still today.

APPLICATION

God's sovereignty extends not merely to weather patterns and viruses and all other parts of creation but to people too. He guides and governs our lives. James, the brother of Jesus, cautions us to be careful in planning out our lives because we do not know what the next day will bring. He goes on to explain, "For you are like a vapor that appears for a little while, then vanishes. Instead, you should say, 'If the Lord wills, we will live and do this or that'" (James 4:14-15). God has full authority and power over every day of our lives. He determines what each day will bring and determines the number of those days (Psalm 90). God's sovereignty does not lead to some kind of bleak determinism; His sovereignty is our comfort. There is hope and joy because, in His sovereignty over us, we can rest in His sovereign care for us.

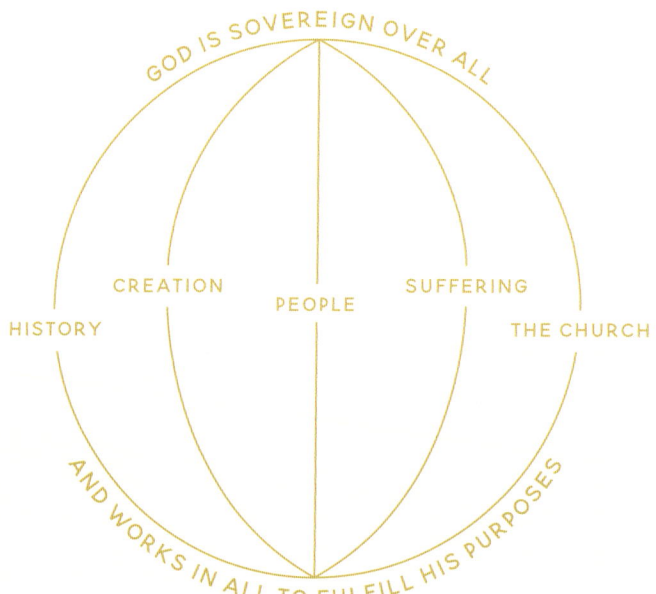

THEOLOGY PROPER *Attributes of God: Sovereign*

Nothing IS OUTSIDE OF HIS CONTROL, AND GOD *sovereignly* WORKS IN *all things* FOR OUR GOOD AND *His glory.*

REVEALED
KNOWLEDGE

THE
KNOWLEDGE
OF GOD

INCOMPREHENSIBLE

God is incomprehensible, which means that although God is knowable, we cannot know Him fully. We will never be able to grasp God perfectly, and we will never stop learning more about His character. The only One who can know God entirely is God Himself. His greatness is unsearchable (Psalm 145:3). No one can understand the depth of His power (Job 26:14). His thoughts and ways are far greater than our thoughts and ways (Isaiah 55:8-9). We study God's attributes to know Him more, but we will never get to a place where we can say we have learned all there is to know about Him. There will always be more. We will understand Him in deeper, richer ways in eternity, but even then, there will be things outside our reach. We can trust that all the things we do not know only add to the abundance of His goodness, for He is good.

APPLICATION

If we were able to know God fully, He would not be God. This would make Him a finite creature, but God is infinite. We, on the other hand, are finite. We have limits, and there are bounds to our characteristics and personality traits. God can fully know us because He sees our every thought, intention, and motive. He knows everything about us. There are even parts of ourselves that we will never fully understand, but God sees the depths of our hearts. And while God knows everything about us — all of our evil intentions and struggles with sin — He still pursued us and redeemed us to Himself. An incomprehensible God desires to be known by people who are limited, broken, and weak. He gives us everything that we need to know about Him in this life in His Word, and we anticipate learning more about Him in the next life..

ROMANS 11:33

Oh, the depth of the riches and the wisdom and the knowledge of God! How unsearchable his judgments and untraceable his ways!

TRANSCENDENT

God is transcendent, which means He is high above us and does not have our same limitations. He is not confined by space, time, or ability. He is exalted and dwells "in heaven above" (Psalm 57:5, Deuteronomy 4:39). As King of kings and Lord of lords, He is in complete control and authority over His world and the people who inhabit it. While God in His transcendence is very much above us in a way we cannot grasp, He is also personal and able to be known by us. These truths seem to be contradictory, but they go hand in hand with each other and display the majesty of God. Our God who dwells in the heavens has also made His dwelling place with man through the Holy Spirit, living inside each believer.

APPLICATION

Skeptics might take the attribute of God's transcendence and infer that because He is beyond us, He is unknowable and should not be trusted. This is the wrong conclusion. Because of God's perfect, just, and good character, we can trust everything about who He is, even the things our finite minds cannot fully comprehend about Him. God's transcendence reminds us that everything about Him is above everything about us. He is God, and we are not. We cannot confine God to human terms and conditions. We cannot apply limited and flawed reasoning to the ways of God. He is above all of our thoughts and all of our ways, and that is a good thing. What human being could have pieced together the story of redemption in which the Creator of the world becomes a man Himself and dies to save His creation, even though they rebelled against Him and rejected fellowship with Him? The transcendence of God calls us to be still and trust in Him and not try to control everything around us. He is above us, and all things are in His hands.

> **GOD IS TRANSCENDENT, WHICH MEANS HE IS HIGH ABOVE US AND DOES NOT HAVE THE SAME LIMITATIONS THAT WE DO.**

THEOLOGY PROPER *Attributes of God: Transcendent, Immanent*

IMMANENT

While God's transcendence speaks to Him being high above all creation, His immanence speaks to His presence within creation. God is not a God who remains above; He is also a God who draws near. Scripture speaks to this truth in Joshua 2:11 when it says, "for the Lord your God is God in heaven above and on earth below." Isaiah 57:15 speaks again to this truth: "I live in a high and holy place, and with the oppressed and lowly of spirit." God's immanence means that He is present and active within the creation He has made. God is not detached from the activity of our world but is involved in it. He is at work with humans and the institutions of our world. God's immanence is ultimately displayed through His Son, Jesus. Jesus is called "Immanuel," which means "God with us." Through Jesus, God's presence came to be among us and save us from sin. God's immanence describes His desire to have an intimate relationship with His creation. He has come near to save us and to bring us into a close relationship with Himself.

APPLICATION

When we meditate on the immanence of the Lord, we become more aware of His presence in our lives. Sometimes we can feel distant from God, but His immanence shows us that He is always with us. Even if we feel far from God, His presence is always near. Because the Holy Spirit dwells within us, we can rest assured that God's presence is always with us. In times of loneliness, we can rest in the constant presence of the Lord. Psalm 34:18 tells us, "The Lord is near to the brokenhearted; he saves those crushed in spirit." Our God is a personal God who desires intimacy with His people. Let this be an encouragement to us when we feel alone or separated from God. God is near.

> **GOD IS NOT A GOD WHO REMAINS ABOVE; HE IS ALSO A GOD WHO DRAWS NEAR.**

GOD IS TRANSCENDENT

GOD IS HIGH ABOVE
SPACE & TIME, MAN'S LIMITATIONS, THOUGHTS, AND FINITE ABILITIES

JOSHUA 2:11B

for the Lord your God is God in heaven above and on earth below.

GOD IS IMMANENT

GOD IS PRESENT AND ACTIVE WITHIN
THE CREATION HE HAS MADE.

THEOLOGY PROPER *Attributes of God: Transcendent, Immanent*

EVEN IF WE FEEL FAR FROM GOD, *His presence is always near.*

THE ANGEL OF THE LORD IN SCRIPTURE

TO HAGAR

Genesis 16:7-13

TO ABRAHAM & SARAH

Genesis 18:1-15

TO ABRAHAM & ISAAC

Genesis 22:9-15

TO JACOB

Genesis 32:24-32

TO MOSES

Exodus 3:1-12

GOD'S PROMISE

Exodus 23:20-23

TO JOSHUA

Joshua 5:13-15

TO GIDEON

Judges 6:11-23

TO SAMSON'S PARENTS

Judges 13:1-22

ANGEL OF THE LORD

The angel of the Lord was a unique manifestation of the Lord's presence in the Old Testament. Though he was given the title, "angel," the angel of the Lord was not like the creatures of God's heavenly court. The Hebrew word translated as "angel" here is *mal'āk*, which means "messenger." Many scholars argue that the angel of the Lord is the preincarnate, second person of the Trinity. Through Scripture, we see the mysterious nature of the angel of the Lord as one that reveals the complexity of God. For example, in Genesis, the angel of the Lord came to Hagar, a woman who was mourning by a spring. He promised to bless her with many children, and Hagar called him *El ro'i*, meaning "the God who sees" (Genesis 16:13). Here, the angel of the Lord was not described as a mouthpiece from God but was God Himself. Furthermore, in Exodus 23:20-21, God told Moses that He would send the Israelites an angel to protect them and lead them to the Promised Land. Giving the angel authority equal to Himself, God declared that this angel would bear the eternal name, *Yahweh*, and must be obeyed. The angel of the Lord was God yet distinct from God and reflected the diverse yet unified nature of God in the Trinity.

APPLICATION

The angel of the Lord pointed to the nature of Jesus Christ. John 1:1 states, "In the beginning was the Word, and the Word was with God, and the Word was God." Jesus Christ, the eternal Word of God, is God yet separate from God the Father. He has existed forever in unity with the Father but is distinct as the Son. In John 10:30, Jesus claims that He and the Father are one, and in John 17:5, Jesus reveals that He and the Father shared glory and authority before the creation of the world. Jesus Christ was the full manifestation of God in flesh and the messenger sent from heaven. With the angel of the Lord in the Old Testament, we see that God planned to redeem us through a relational being. This truth culminated in the work of Jesus Christ. Jesus descended to accomplish the redemptive work planned for Him.

Like the angel of the Lord who came near Hagar, Jesus came near us to comfort us through sorrow and bless us with His presence. Through His obedient life, death, and resurrection, He forgave us of our sin and restored us to have a relationship with the Father. And, by the Spirit of Jesus living within us through faith, we know that God is always near us. When we are in times of distress, the Holy Spirit brings relief and wisdom. There is no place we can try to run that the Messenger of God does not know; Jesus will find us anywhere we are. We can pray for the peaceful presence of God and be sure that He will carry us through our days.

THEOPHANY

A theophany is the physical manifestation of God to humans. God appears as theophanies in Scripture in different ways, either in the form of an angel, man, or something in nature. Being an invisible God, we should not misunderstand theophanies to be the form of how God actually looks. Instead, they are God taking the form of something to communicate with people. A Christophany refers to an appearance of Christ, specifically the preincarnate Christ. Typically, God makes theophanies in Scripture in a visual display, such as the burning bush in Exodus 3 or the cloud of fire that led the Israelites in Exodus 14:19. Theophanies often include sounds and other creative elements. For example, in Ezekial's vision of the Lord in Ezekiel 1, his description of the appearance of God is seen by a cloud with brightness around it, a flashing fire, and the voice of God sounding like a mighty army. God uses theophanies to communicate an aspect of His nature and character. The booming of thunder and the mightiness of the wind can describe the power of God, or a vision of Him on His throne can describe His rule and reign. Theophanies are also often used to accompany a prophecy or an occurrence of rescue or judgment.

APPLICATION

We should not breeze past theophanies in Scripture. A theophany helps us understand who God is by looking at creative elements that we are used to seeing in everyday life. Visual and audible displays like lights and sounds in Scripture should cause us to be in awe of our great God. Nothing in our human understanding can come close to fully describing the nature of God, but we can still allow the grandeur of fire or the rumbling of thunder to lead us to worship the glory of God. As we come across theophanies in Scripture, we should take the time to notice what God is using and how He uses that particular thing to describe His character and His relationship with mankind. Such revelation allows us to know our God uniquely, and we should be excited to learn more about Him in this way.

> **A THEOPHANY HELPS US UNDERSTAND WHO GOD IS BY LOOKING AT CREATIVE ELEMENTS THAT WE ARE USED TO SEEING IN EVERYDAY LIFE.**

THEOPHANIES IN SCRIPTURE

THE BURNING BUSH
Exodus 3

A CLOUD
Exodus 16:10

THUNDER & FIRE
Exodus 19:18-19

TORNADO
Job 38:1

SMOKE
Exodus 20:18

PROVIDENCE

God sovereignly rules and oversees the world, but He is also active within the workings of the world. God's providence refers to how God preserves and governs His purposes for creation. Through His providence, God both foresees what will happen and acts to make those events come to be. God's work of preservation through His providence means that God actively maintains His creation. Because God controls His creation, He preserves His creation by protecting it and keeping it stable. We can also see God's preservation in the lives of His creatures. For example, God continued to preserve the people of Israel throughout the Old Testament even when they faced danger and exile. Another aspect of God's providence is His governance. This means God actively works in creation to accomplish His purposes. Like a governor who has authority over his or her state to direct plans, God authoritatively orchestrates events for His plans and purposes. Everything we see around us occurs because of God's providential hand. There are no random occurrences or chances, for God orchestrates all things purposefully.

APPLICATION

God's providence leads us to trust in God's plans. Knowing that God holds everything in His hands gives us comfort when we are troubled by the circumstances around us. God's providence encourages us because He uses everything, even the hard things, to accomplish His will. We can hold our plans loosely and trust God with open hands knowing that He is in control. When we are worried, God's providence reminds us that He is taking care of us and will provide for us. His providence also leads us to rejoice over His activity within creation. Without the Lord's providence, our world would be in disorder, but by His grace, He preserves every part of creation. Nothing is outside His hands.

> **THROUGH HIS PROVIDENCE, GOD BOTH FORESEES WHAT WILL HAPPEN AND ACTS TO MAKE THOSE EVENTS COME TO BE.**

IN THIS SECTION

Inspiration of Scripture

Inerrancy of Scripture

Sufficiency of Scripture

Eternality of Scripture

Canon

Original Languages of Scripture

Bible Translations

Bibliology

THE STUDY OF THE BIBLE

QUESTIONS ANSWERED

What is the Bible? | *Where did the Bible come from?* | *Can I trust the Bible?*
What impact does the Bible have on my life?

THE WORD OF GOD IS *living and active.*

INSPIRATION OF SCRIPTURE

The inspiration of Scripture means that the Bible is the Word of God. It is not merely a beautiful work of art whose renown has endured throughout the ages like Homer's *Iliad*. While the Bible has withstood the test of time, and its accuracy has been affirmed by more ancient manuscripts than any other piece of writing, the Bible is different because God inspired it. It is not a product of men (1 Thessalonians 2:13) but is the living oracles of God (Acts 7:38). The Words of Scripture are "breathed out" by God (2 Timothy 3:16 ESV). While God employed over forty men with unique writing styles and perspectives to pen the words of Scripture, He provided the content. The inspiration of Scripture is why the Bible is authoritative as the standard of truth for all of life's principles. It is the only book that has divine authority because it is the very Word of God.

APPLICATION

Because the Bible is the inspired Word of God, it is powerful. The words of Scripture do not just move us like great works of poetry or captivating stories. The Word of God is living and active, and it can "judge the thoughts and intentions of the heart" (Hebrews 4:12). It exposes the truth to us, revealing our sins and the way of salvation. As believers, we then feast on God's living words, day in and day out. It is our daily bread. Our souls are nourished; our deepest thirst is quenched. We find that His Word produces a change in us as the Spirit uses it to grow us in Christlikeness. We read, study, meditate on, and memorize Scripture, knowing that it is the primary means through which God speaks to us. He reveals His character and shows us His glory, and we come to know Him through our Bible intake. In turn, our love for Him grows! Our love then fuels our obedience, and we find that as we align our lives to biblical truths and principles, we experience perfect joy and delight (Luke 11:28).

> **THE INSPIRATION OF SCRIPTURE IS WHY THE BIBLE IS AUTHORITATIVE AS THE STANDARD OF TRUTH FOR ALL OF LIFE'S PRINCIPLES.**

EUROPE

LUKE
MARK
PAUL

PAUL

JOHN

AFRICA

THE INSPIRED WORD OF GOD

GOD USED **40 DIFFERENT MEN** FROM **3 DIFFERENT CONTINENTS** ACROSS A TIME SPAN OF **1,500 YEARS** TO WRITE HIS WORD.

BIBLIOLOGY *Inspiration of Scripture*

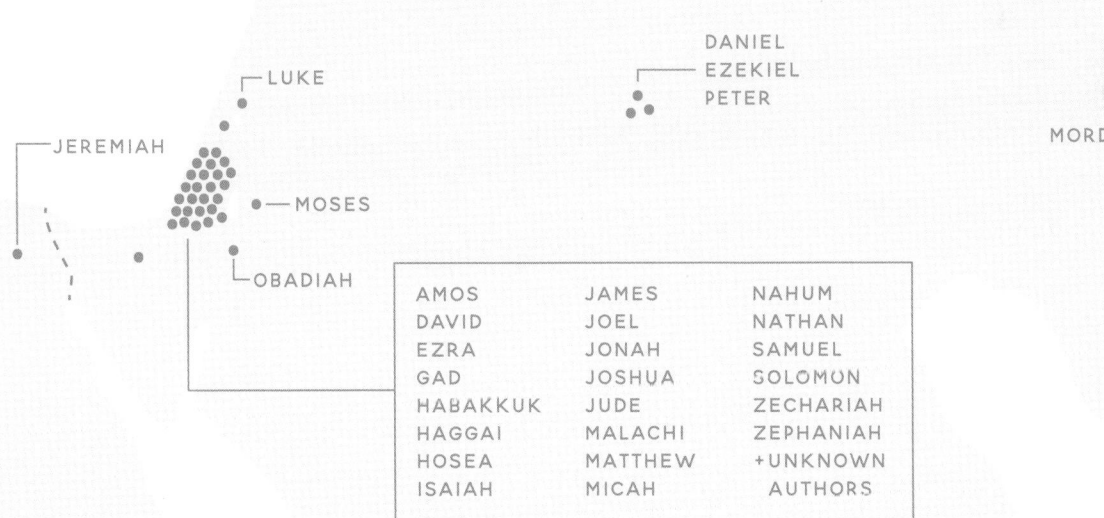

ASIA

JEREMIAH

LUKE

MOSES

OBADIAH

DANIEL
EZEKIEL
PETER

MORDECAI

AMOS	JAMES	NAHUM
DAVID	JOEL	NATHAN
EZRA	JONAH	SAMUEL
GAD	JOSHUA	SOLOMON
HABAKKUK	JUDE	ZECHARIAH
HAGGAI	MALACHI	ZEPHANIAH
HOSEA	MATTHEW	+UNKNOWN
ISAIAH	MICAH	AUTHORS

INERRANCY OF SCRIPTURE

The doctrine of inerrancy teaches that the Bible is without error. It states that the original manuscripts are without discrepancies or contradictions of any kind because the Bible is the Word of God. To claim that the Bible contains error would imply an error in God since the Bible is His Word. Error is either a mistake stemming from imperfection or a lie stemming from deception, but there can be no imperfection in God, for He is completely holy and perfect. Numbers 23:19 states, "God is not a man, that he might lie, or a son of man, that he might change his mind. Does he speak and not act, or promise and not fulfill?" Unlike humans who regularly make mistakes, God's perfection reveals His incapability to blunder. Because He is without error, His Word is without error.

APPLICATION

Because the Bible is inerrant, it is completely trustworthy. In a world flooded with opposing versions of the truth, we have the truth of God's authoritative Word to ground us. Because God's Word is accurate, we can believe what it says about the reality of our sin and the means for our salvation with absolute certainty. If the Bible were not true, then the gospel message would not be true, ultimately leaving us without any means for salvation. We can have confidence in the truth of the gospel as believers because the Word of God declares it to be so. The inerrancy of Scripture also allows a place to rest the doubts we may have, knowing and believing that the truthfulness of His Word covers them. It declares that God is who He says He is, and He will do what He has promised to do. His character is to be trusted. The Bible is to be trusted more than any person, ideology, or organization, and the truths found within it should be the foundation of our worldview. Whenever we form beliefs or convictions, we should not fail to test them against the Word of God. Christ said that "the Scripture cannot be broken" (John 10:35); we can depend on the unchanging, unerring Word of God.

THERE CAN BE NO IMPERFECTION IN GOD, FOR HE IS COMPLETELY HOLY AND PERFECT.

BIBLIOGY *Inerrancy of Scripture*

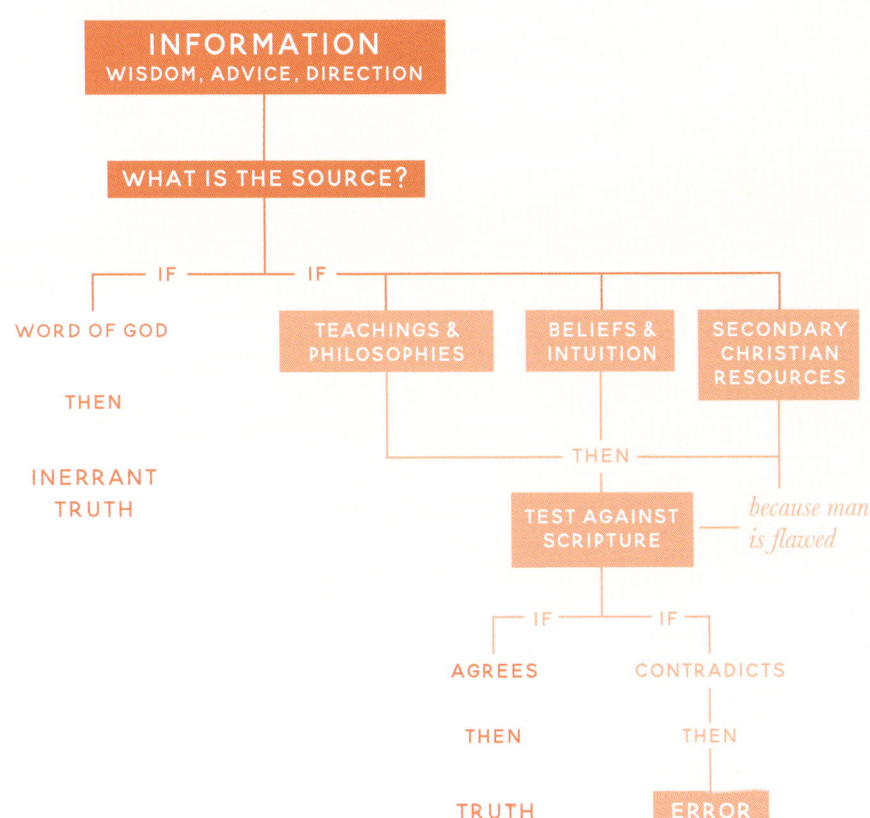

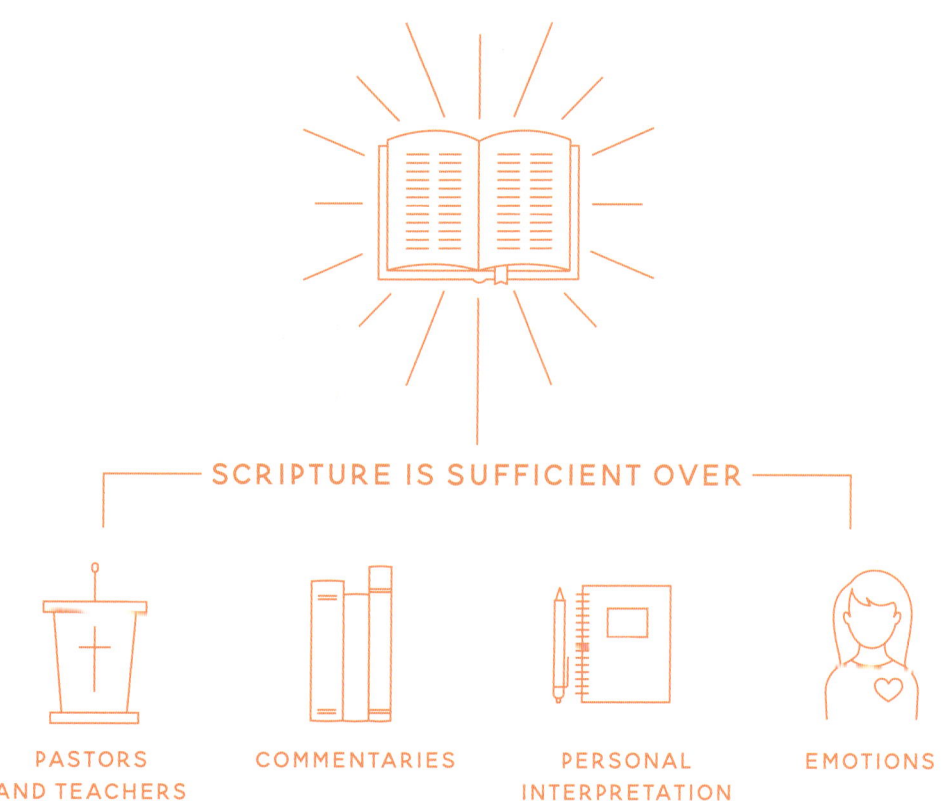

SUFFICIENCY OF SCRIPTURE

The sufficiency of Scripture means that the Bible communicates everything we need to know about God, salvation, and how to live godly lives in light of the gospel. We do not need to search for a new revelation from God outside of Scripture because He has already revealed Himself in the Bible. The sufficiency of Scripture does not mean that any other source apart from the Bible is useless—we can benefit from theologians, pastors, and commentaries to help us understand the Bible—but they are not our final authority. Only Scripture has the final say in the believer's life as Scripture is grounded in God and His perfect, unchanging character (Psalm 19:7, Hebrews 13:8).

APPLICATION

The truth of the sufficiency of Scripture means that everything we need for life and godliness is written in the Bible (2 Peter 1:3). It contains sufficient principles to guide us in every thought, decision, and situation. It is truly our most valuable possession. Because Scripture is sufficient, we do not need to look for a new revelation or wait for God to communicate new insight through our feelings. He has spoken to us through His Word. We also do not need to immerse ourselves in the latest personality test or self-help book to grow. We can walk in confidence and peace in the truth and sufficiency of Scripture and let its wisdom and riches become more dear to us than life itself (Colossians 3:16). It can make us more like Christ each time we read it, and it is the final authority over every decision we make.

2 PETER 1:3

His divine power has given us everything required for life and godliness through the knowledge of him who called us by his own glory and goodness

ETERNALITY OF SCRIPTURE

Scripture is eternal, which means that the Bible's truths are unchanging, timeless, and everlasting. Isaiah 40:8 declares, "The grass withers, the flowers fade, but the word of our God remains forever." The prophet Isaiah applauds the eternality of God's speech over the passing world, highlighting that the revelation of God through His Word is unchanging and everlasting. Whatever God speaks will come to pass and will remain true. Scripture is eternal because God is eternal, and the Bible is His Word. All of Scripture points to God's eternal plan to redeem His people and shows its fulfillment in the coming Savior.

APPLICATION

Cultural trends, social movements, and fad diets come and go. Material possessions, people, accolades, and wealth are here one moment and gone the next. But God's Word alone stands. His timeless Word is also relevant and convicting, giving us wisdom for each area or season of life. Whether we are in school, at home, or in the workplace, God offers biblical wisdom so that we can cling to what is everlasting: the saving knowledge of Jesus Christ. Through faith in the Word of God, we are forgiven of our sins and are gifted with eternality in the likeness of our Savior and Maker. Until we reach eternity with God in heaven, we preach as prophets in this world, speaking the eternal words of God and calling others to see the constant and surpassing truth of Jesus.

> SCRIPTURE IS ETERNAL BECAUSE GOD IS ETERNAL, AND THE BIBLE IS HIS WORD.

BIBLIOGRAPHY *Eternality of Scripture*

The grass withers, the flowers fade, but the word of our God remains forever

ISAIAH 40:8

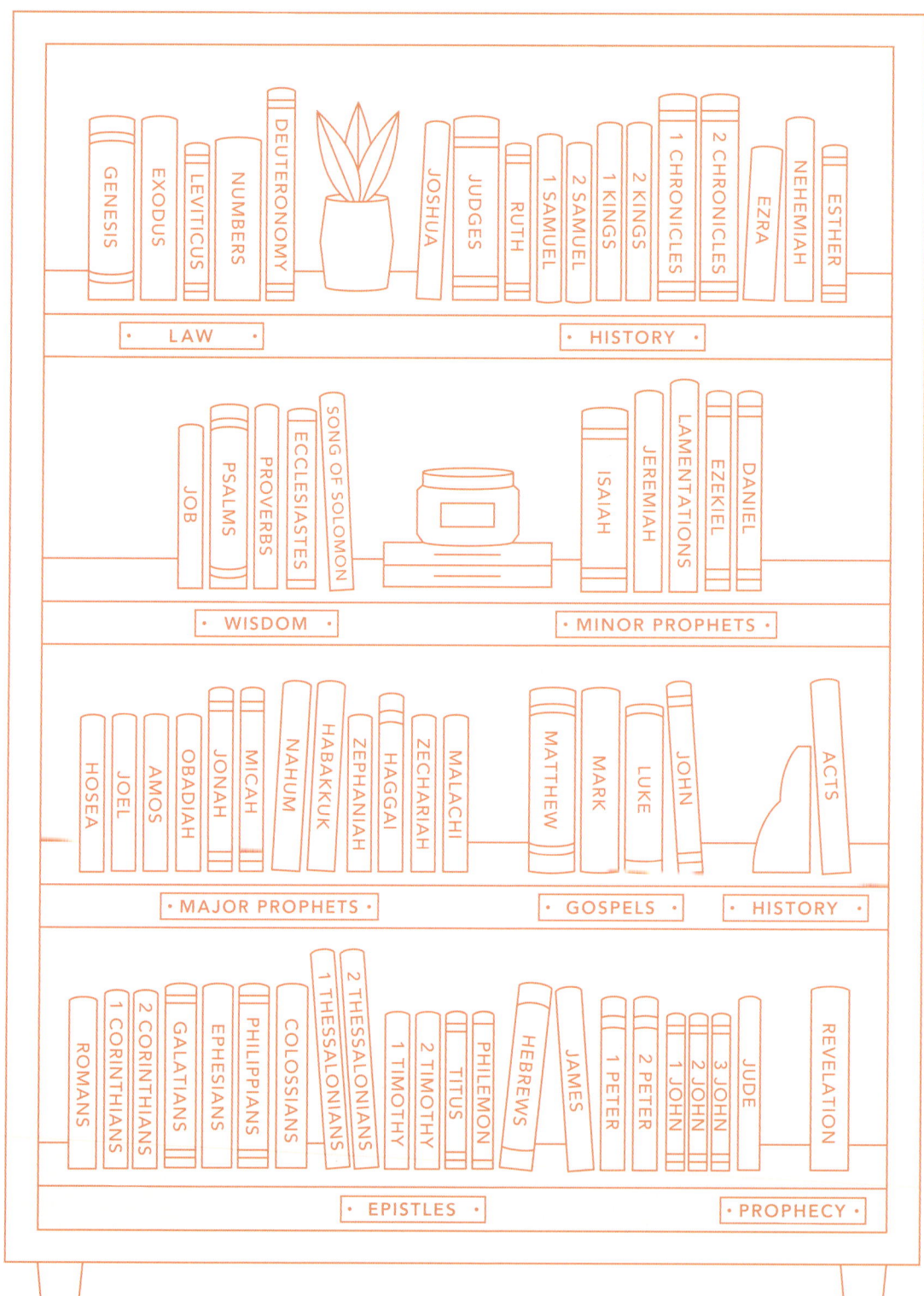

CANON

The canon of Scripture refers to the sixty-six books of the Bible. The word "canon" is from the Greek word *kanón*, which means "rule" or "standard." There are thirty-nine books in the Old Testament containing the Hebrew laws, prophets, and writings. The New Testament consists of twenty-seven books, all written by apostles of Jesus or their close associates within roughly one hundred years of His death. These books were compiled and later affirmed as the authoritative Word of God during the Council of Hippo (AD 393) and the Council of Carthage (AD 397). It is important to note that men did not make Scripture authoritative, for the Bible was God's inerrant Word from the moment it was penned. Rather, these councils affirmed, or ratified, which books were already the holy, inspired writings of God.

HOW WERE THE BOOKS SELECTED?

The Council of Hippo and Council of Carthage used strict criteria during the canonization process. Scholars ensured that the early local church affirmed each book, that the books reflected evidence and internal qualities of the Holy Spirit, and that they were consistent with the rest of Scripture. Additionally, every New Testament book needed to be directly connected with one of the apostles. This is why the death of the last apostle meant that the canon was closed. Furthermore, Jesus affirmed the Old Testament books as authoritative (Matthew 23:35, Luke 24:44, Luke 11:45-51), and almost all of the Old Testament books are referenced within New Testament writings. The complete canon was formalized by the early church and is now closed, meaning no additional books can be added or taken away from it. Every word of the Bible is God-breathed, authoritative, and inspired (2 Timothy 3:16-17).

APPLICATION

God has revealed Himself to us through the Word, and from the canon, we learn about who He is and why we exist. Through the Bible, we become aware of God's holiness, our sinfulness, and our need for a Savior. We also learn how to live lives that reflect His grace by protecting the weak, pursuing integrity, and loving one another. The closed nature of the canon reminds us that we are not waiting on another "word from the Lord" or another hidden manuscript for additional revelation. God has not given secret knowledge to a select few holy men. He has spoken everything that we need for life and godliness through His finished Word, and no one should add to or take away from the Words of Scripture. Through the canonized Bible, God has revealed Himself to us so that we can know Him and live godly lives.

CRITERIA FOR CANONIZATION
NEW TESTAMENT BOOKS

 AFFIRMED BY THE EARLY LOCAL CHURCH

 REFLECTS THE POWER OF GOD TO COMFORT, INSTRUCT, CORRECT, AND CONVICT

 CONSISTENT WITH THE REST OF SCRIPTURE

 APOSTOLICITY: WRITTEN BY AN APOSTLE OR A CLOSE ASSOCIATE

BIBLIOGY *Canon*

EVERY WORD OF THE BIBLE IS *God-breathed, authoritative,* AND *inspired.*

ORIGINAL LANGUAGES OF SCRIPTURE

(Hebrew, Koine Greek, Aramaic)

The original languages of Scripture fall into one of three languages. Nearly all of the Old Testament is written in Hebrew, and the New Testament is written in the form of Greek widely understood 2,000 years ago in the Mediterranean. This form of the Greek language is Koine Greek. The third language, which is often overlooked, is Aramaic. Aramaic was the dominant spoken language when Hebrew was a regional language spoken only by people in Jerusalem, and Greek was not as widely used in the Mediterranean. Aramaic was the language used by Jesus's mother and those who surrounded Him. The books in the Old Testament that are not written in Hebrew—which include a few chapters in the books of Ezra and Daniel and a few miscellaneous passages and verses throughout the rest of the Bible—are written in Aramaic.

APPLICATION

A proper understanding of Scripture requires consideration for the original Hebrew, Koine Greek, and Aramaic to find the most accurate depiction of its original, intended meaning. While some may have the opportunity to learn these languages, we can benefit from concordances, commentaries, and other tools that help us to understand the original meaning of the text. What great appreciation and gratitude we should have for those who have exhausted such time and effort in studying and translating the original languages of the Bible into common languages so that we can read God's Word today.

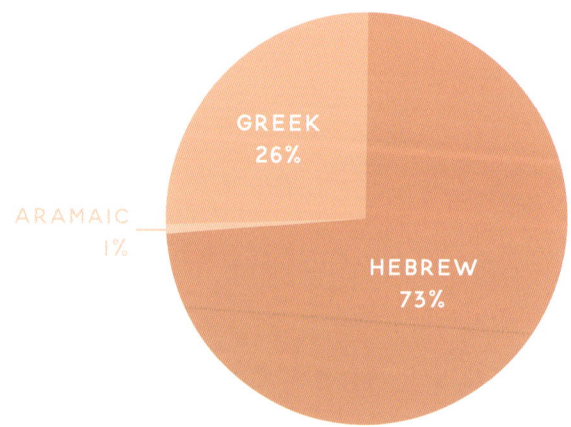

* Percentage based on total number of verses in the Bible. Values are rounded.

BIBLIOGY *Original Languages*

DEUTERONOMY 6:4 - HEBREW

שְׁמַע יִשְׂרָאֵל יְהוָה אֱלֹהֵינוּ יְהוָה אֶחָד:

Listen, Israel: The Lord our God, the Lord is one.

DANIEL 2:20 - ARAMAIC

עָנֵה דָנִיֵּאל וְאָמַר לֶהֱוֵא שְׁמֵהּ דִּי־אֱלָהָא מְבָרַךְ מִן־עָלְמָא וְעַד־עָלְמָא דִּי חָכְמְתָא וּגְבוּרְתָא דִּי לֵהּ־הִיא:

May the name of God be praised forever and ever, for wisdom and power belong to him.

JOHN 1:1 - GREEK

ἐν ἀρχῇ ἦν ὁ λόγος καὶ ὁ λόγος ἦν πρὸς τὸν θεόν καὶ θεὸς ἦν ὁ λόγος

In the beginning was the Word, and the Word was with God, and the Word was God.

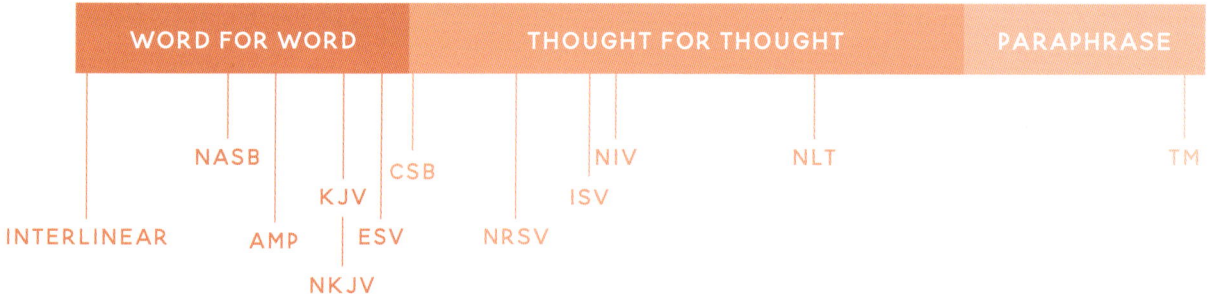

COMPARISON OF BIBLE TRANSLATIONS

NASB *North American Standard Bible*
AMP *Amplified Bible*
KJV *King James Version*
NKJV *New King James Version*
ESV *English Standard Version*
CSB *Christian Standard Bible*
NRSV *New Revised Standard Version*
ISV *International Standard Version*
NIV *New International Version*
NLT *New Living Translation*
TM *The Message*

BIBLE TRANSLATIONS

Having access to so many translations of the Bible is a privilege. Yet, it can also prove to be a challenge when deciding which translation we want to use. It is important to understand the process of Bible translation. First, there is the word for word translation. This approach seeks to present the original languages in a more literal translation, word for word, to preserve as much of the original textual emphasis as possible. This type of translation is used in Bible versions like the King James Version, New American Standard Version, and English Standard Version. Another process is referred to as thought for thought translation. This approach emphasizes the meaning of the passage, so the thoughts are understandable to the reader. This type of translation seeks to present the ideas of the original text in a way that is accessible to the common reader, and accurately represents idiomatic expressions that we might not understand word for word. Examples of thought for thought versions of the Bible include the New International Version and the Christian Standard Bible. Some Bible translations fall under the category of paraphrase, such as The Message.

APPLICATION

The hope for each Bible translation is to present God's Word in a way that is both accurate and easily understood by the reader. We will likely be drawn to one translation over the others, and that may sometimes even depend on your setting and what you are doing with your reading. A more literal translation may be more helpful when studying the Bible more in-depth or preparing to teach from Scripture. A less literal translation may be more preferred for day-to-day or devotional reading. It may even be helpful to compare translations by using them alongside one another. In any case, we can praise God for those who have faithfully provided us with many translations of the Bible, providing us the ability to read and understand God's Word today.

IN THIS SECTION

Image of God

Creation Mandate

What is Sin?

The Fall

Original Sin

Condemnation

Total Depravity

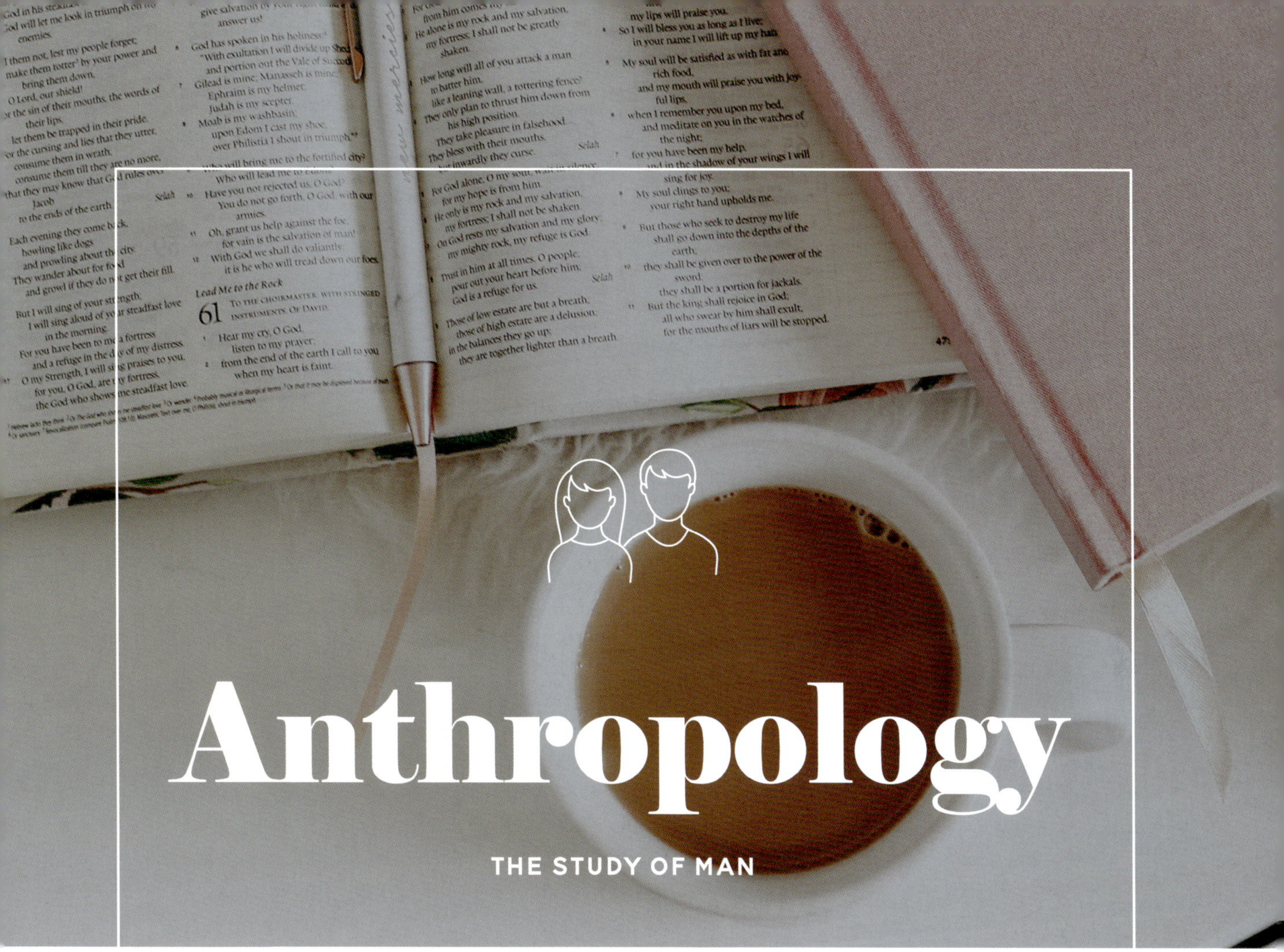

Anthropology

THE STUDY OF MAN

QUESTIONS ANSWERED

How does God relate to humans? | *How are humans different from animals?*
Are people naturally good or evil?

IMAGE OF GOD

When God created humans, He made them in His image, or in the *imago Dei*. As the culminating act of creation, God created mankind to mirror His nature and be His representatives on the earth, making humans different from animals. In the garden of Eden, God gave humanity a state of "original righteousness" that was untested. When Adam and Eve sinned, the image of God in humanity was marred but not lost, and all mankind is still "made in God's likeness" (James 3:9). The extent of this likeness is multi-dimensional. All mankind has a rational and moral nature, including the ability to engage the intellect, experience complex emotions, and exercise moral judgments. We each have a conscience along with a spiritual capacity to relate to God and an awareness of the distant future that extends to eternity (Ecclesiastes 3:11). Though God does not have a body as we do, our ability to procreate and bear children who are like us is also a reflection of God and His work of creation (Genesis 5:3).

In order to see the untarnished image of God, we must look to Jesus Christ, who is the perfect "image of the invisible God" (Colossians 1:15, Hebrews 1:3). Christ alone wholly embodied moral perfection, and it is through our union with Him that the original righteousness that was lost to sin can be regained. In Him, we can know God and grow in righteousness and holiness through the power of the Holy Spirit and obedience to His Word. The power of sin is broken, and by His grace, we can be conformed to the image of Christ, putting His character and moral purity on display more and more (2 Corinthians 3:18). This process of sanctification will be complete when Christ returns, and "we will be like him because we will see him as he is" (1 John 3:2).

APPLICATION

Because God created all humans in His image, all people are worthy of dignity and respect. Though sin has marred the image of God in all people, believers can fight sin and overcome it through the power of the Holy Spirit working inside them. Through the process of sanctification—becoming more and more like Christ—God's image in us as believers is restored as we grow to reflect His holiness, love, goodness, mercy, faithfulness, and patience. We place His glory on display as image-bearers of Christ. And as His image-bearers, we should readily acknowledge the inherent value of all mankind and offer equal dignity and respect to all, regardless of ethnicity, socioeconomic status, or prestige.

ANTHROPOLOGY *Image of God*

IMAGO DEI

RATIONAL & MORAL NATURE
Intellect, Emotions, Judgments

CONSCIENCE & SPIRITUAL CAPACITY
Ability to relate to God
Awareness of eternity

PARENTING & MAKING DISCIPLES
Reflection of God's work of creation

THE CREATION MANDATE

GOD BLESSED THEM

→ BE FRUITFUL & MULTIPLY

IN DOING SO MAN REFLECTS HOW GOD:

created the world & filled it with good things

→ SUBDUE THE EARTH & HAVE DOMINION OVER IT

IN DOING SO MAN REFLECTS HOW GOD:

rules over and cares for all creation

CREATION MANDATE

When God created Adam and Eve in His image, He gave them commands to uphold as His representative on the earth. These commands are collectively called the creation mandate or the cultural mandate. The first element of the mandate in Genesis 1:28 is God's blessing of humanity. The commands in themselves are a blessing, and it is in response to God's blessing that mankind was to obey. Next, God commanded humans to mirror His creative work through the call to be fruitful and multiply. Just as God created the world and filled it with good things, God wanted mankind to procreate and fill the world with more image-bearers. Finally, the cultural mandate includes the command to subdue the earth and have dominion over it. God rules over all creation, and as His representatives, humans were to rule over the planet, tending to it and taking care of it.

APPLICATION

As God's image-bearers, we are called to reflect His character and His work in the world. We can do this as we center our actions—how we live—on Christ. In His Word, He calls us to obey His commandments, and as we do so, we grow to become more and more like Him. However, our call does not end there. As we grow through that sanctification process, we fulfill the creation mandate as we are fruitful and multiply, whether through parenting or following the command that Jesus gives us in Matthew 28:19 to go and "make disciples of all nations." As Christ's disciples, we are to spread throughout the earth through global missions or by making disciples right where He has us—as parents, teachers, or involved citizens in our communities. In this way, we share the message of Christ with others, furthering the spread of the gospel through every avenue that we can for as long as we are able.

> THE COMMANDS IN THEMSELVES ARE A BLESSING, AND IT IS IN RESPONSE TO GOD'S BLESSING THAT MANKIND WAS TO OBEY.

WHAT IS SIN?

Sin is disobeying or not fulfilling God's law. When many people hear the word "sin," they think of the Ten Commandments, which include commands like "Do not murder," "Do not commit adultery," and "Do not steal" (Exodus 20:13-15). While these actions do indeed violate God's righteous requirements, Jesus took these commands a step further. He said that it is a sin not only to steal or murder but also to covet or foster hate in our hearts (Matthew 5:21-22). We sin when we disobey God's law with our bodies, thoughts, hearts, emotions, and nature. When we lust, lie, cheat, or steal, we violate God's holy commands. God, who sees all, knows every thought, attitude, and action that does not conform to His will. We can do no good thing apart from Him. Finally, in 1 John 3:4, we read that "sin is lawlessness," and the penalty for sin is death (Romans 6:23).

APPLICATION

Whether due to our own sin or the sin of someone else, we all feel the effects of sin in the world. Throughout our lives, we may suffer abuse, addiction, or divorce. Many of us experience things like slander, conflict, or betrayal. The world is broken by sin, and we are desperately in need of a Savior. Thankfully, God has created a way for us to be right with Him by sending His Son. Jesus Christ, who is fully God and fully man, bore our sins on the cross and destroyed its power over us. For all who believe in Jesus, Christ took our sins upon Himself and gave us His righteousness. Jesus paid the full penalty of death so that all who believe would be saved.

The mystery and the beauty of the gospel are that God loves broken and rebellious sinners who openly hate Him. God calls and adopts sinners as His children, and He pours out His extravagant grace upon them. Yet, while we have been set free from the power and penalty of sin, its presence still remains. As Christians, we are called to mourn over our sin. We are called to fight off sin and resist temptation by the power of the Spirit, choosing to obey God rather than our own sinful desires. One day, when Jesus comes again, there will be no more sin, brokenness, or death. He will wipe it out forever, and we will live for all of eternity at peace with God.

ANTHROPOLOGY *What is Sin?*

SIN: A MATTER OF THE HEART
Matthew 5

WHAT THE LAW SAYS	WHAT CHRIST SAYS
Do not murder (v. 21).	Do not be angry with a brother or sister.
Do not commit adultery (v. 27).	Do not look on a woman lustfully.
Divorce requires a notice of divorce (v. 31).	Divorce causes adultery. (exception: cases of sexual immorality)
Do not break your oaths (v. 33).	Let your 'yes' mean 'yes' and your 'no' mean 'no.'
An eye for an eye and a tooth for a tooth (v. 38).	Turn the other cheek.
Love your neighbor (v. 43).	Love your enemies.

EFFECTS OF THE FALL

- WORK
- THE EARTH
- RELATIONSHIPS
- EMOTIONS
- PHYSICAL BODY
- PARENTING
- CHILDBEARING
- MARRIAGE

THE FALL

The fall occurred in Genesis 3 when Adam and Eve succumbed to temptation and fell into sin. In this account, the serpent successfully tempted Adam and Eve to eat the fruit of the one tree God prohibited. Adam and Eve dismissed God's command and ate the fruit, and human sin was introduced into the world. Because of this sin, their fellowship with God was broken. The consequence of Adam and Eve's disobedience held a curse with far-reaching effects (Genesis 3:17) as chaos and disorder took their place in creation. From that point forward, all generations of their offspring, including each one of us today, would be inclined toward sin and evil. Paul writes that many were made sinners through one man's disobedience (Romans 5:19), and because death was introduced through Adam, all suffer the consequences of sin (1 Corinthians 15:22). Not only is mankind cursed by the effects of the fall, but so is creation as a whole. Creation now groans and waits in longing for restoration—looking forward to that day we will escape the curse of sin (Romans 8:19-23) when Christ returns.

APPLICATION

The effects of the fall are deadly. Because of our inherited sin, all of humanity deserves death and separation from God, both earthly and eternally (Romans 3:23, 6:23). We not only earn consequences of separation from God and the destruction of sin while we live in the world, but we also earn separation from Him in eternity in hell. Without another way and left to ourselves, we are hopeless and depraved. The world would continue in complete chaos and disorder, ruled by sin and evil. But our compassionate and merciful God does not leave us helpless in this state. He provides another way. Immediately following the acts of disobedience recorded in Genesis 3, He offers hope—a promise of a plan for redemption and restoration through His incarnate Son, Jesus Christ. For in His Son's perfect life, death, and resurrection, God reverses the curse of sin for all who place their faith and hope in Christ. Jesus's death and resurrection were part of God's plan from the beginning to restore the whole of creation and defeat death in final victory.

ORIGINAL SIN

The doctrine of original sin teaches that human sin and death find their origin in Adam's sin. Adam served as the representative for all of humanity, and what is true of a representative is true of those he represents. Because of Adam's sin in the garden, all people have inherited a sinful nature and are guilty before the Lord. Romans 5:12 says, "Therefore, just as sin entered the world through one man, and death through sin, in this way death spread to all people, because all sinned." When Adam and Eve disobeyed God in the garden of Eden, they committed the first human sin and brought with it a curse for all humanity. Because of this, every person is born with a sinful nature. We are born under the curse of the law, morally corrupt and stuck in our sin, unable to save ourselves (Galatians 3:13). Just as Adam and Eve were cast out of the garden and separated from a holy God, we too are separated from God because of our sin.

APPLICATION

Because of original sin, all are sinful and, in consequence, deserve death. Apart from Christ, there are no morally good people. We are helpless to save ourselves, but in Jesus Christ, we have a better representative. Jesus is the only sinless human ever to live, and when we trust in Him, He is our representative instead of Adam. What is true of the representative is true of us, so those who trust in Christ no longer bear the guilt of sin but the righteousness of Jesus. Romans 5:17 says, "If by the one man's trespass, death reigned through that one man, how much more will those who receive the overflow of grace and the gift of righteousness reign in life through the one man, Jesus Christ." Adam's sinful nature may have been given to us, but when we put our faith in Jesus Christ, His righteousness is given to us by grace through faith. He is our new representative; He is the better Adam. His perfect righteousness covers the penalty of our sin, and we are free from punishment. While believers still experience the battle of sin, we are no longer guilty in the eyes of God.

> WE ARE HELPLESS TO SAVE OURSELVES, BUT IN JESUS CHRIST, WE HAVE A BETTER REPRESENTATIVE.

ANTHROPOLOGY *Original Sin*

FEDERAL HEADSHIP

Under a covenant, the people are represented by a federal head or covenant head. What is true of the representative is true of the people. Apart from Christ, Adam is our representative, but if we put our faith in Christ, He is our representative.

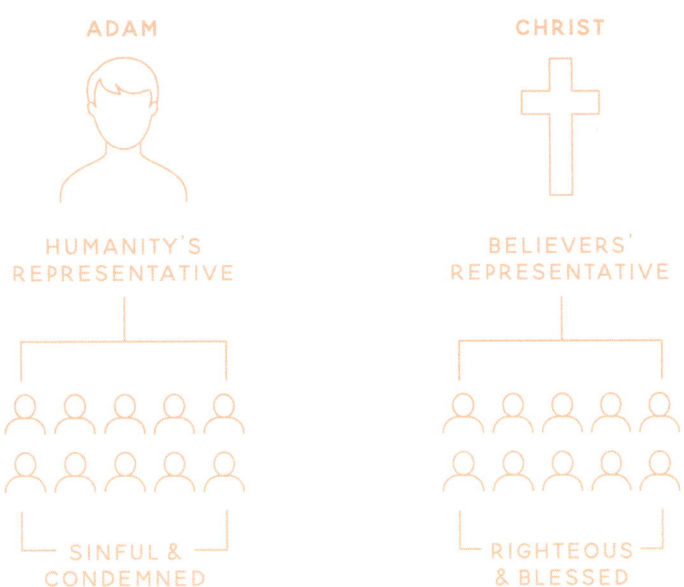

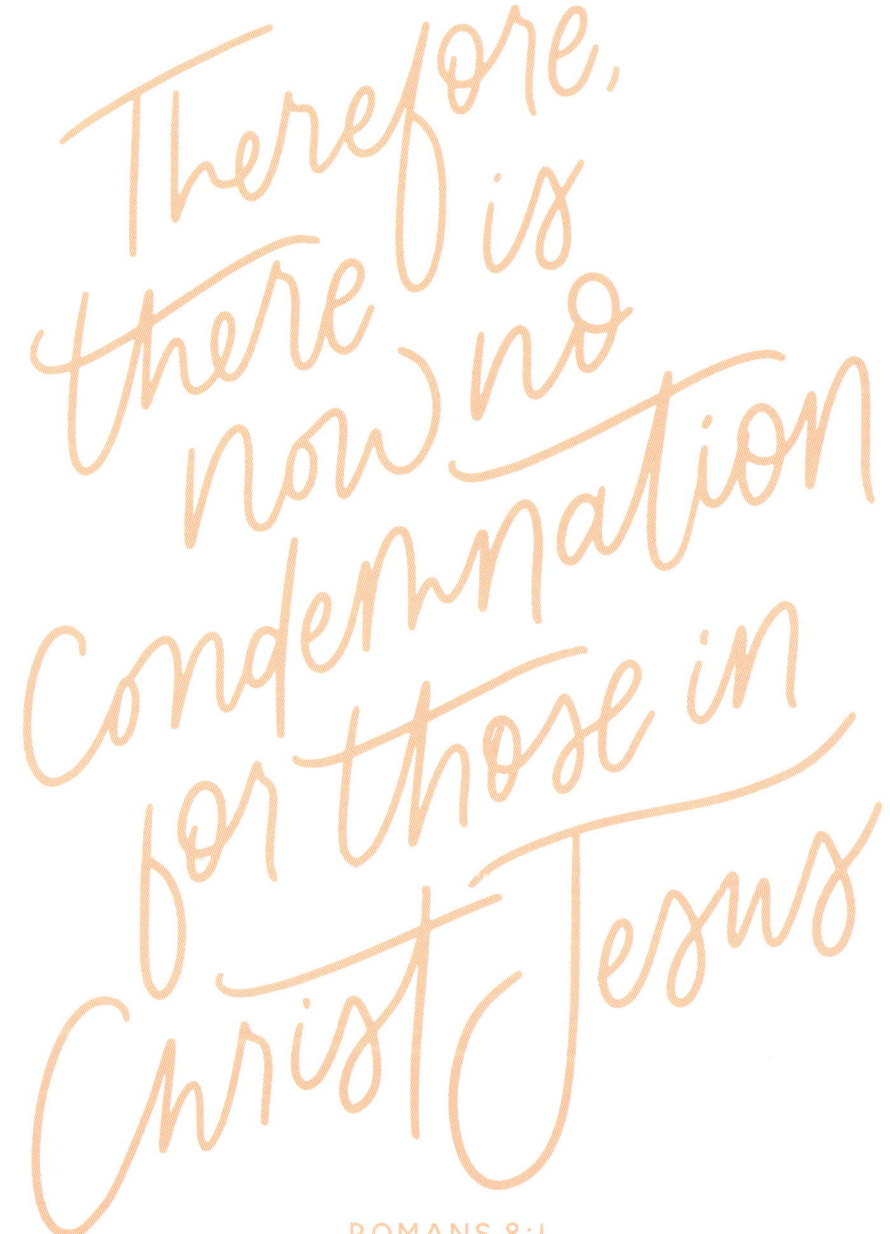

Therefore, there is now no condemnation for those in Christ Jesus

ROMANS 8:1

CONDEMNATION

Condemnation is the act of holding someone accountable for wrongful actions. Like a criminal declared guilty faces consequences for his wrongdoings, God justly brings judgment on sin. The punishment for sin is death. Every single one of us is sinful and therefore condemned to death for our sin. There is only one means by which we can be justified, and that is through salvation in Jesus Christ. When Jesus died on the cross, He stood before the judge and took our place. He stood condemned, bearing the wrath and punishment of God so we can stand vindicated, set free from the punishment we deserve.

APPLICATION

Through the sacrifice of Jesus Christ, condemnation now has no place in the life of the believer. Jesus has already stood condemned in our place and now stands as our advocate, face to face with God, pleading our case (1 John 2:1-2). Because Jesus took our punishment upon Himself, He gives perfect righteousness to all who find salvation in Him. Through confession and repentance, trusting Christ as our Savior, God is faithful and just to forgive and cleanse us from all unrighteousness (1 John 1:9). Paul declares this freedom from condemnation in Romans 8:33-34: "Who can bring an accusation against God's elect? God is the one who justifies. Who is the one who condemns? Christ Jesus is the one who died, but even more, has been raised; he also is at the right hand of God and intercedes for us." As Christians, we will never stand condemned before our Savior.

> THROUGH THE SACRIFICE OF JESUS CHRIST, CONDEMNATION NOW HAS NO PLACE IN THE LIFE OF THE BELIEVER.

TOTAL DEPRAVITY

The doctrine of total depravity flows from the doctrine of original sin. Ever since Adam and Eve committed the first sin in the garden, every human being has been born into sin and is affected by evil in some way. All of us are wholly depraved in our sinful nature. This means that our fallenness affects everything about us—our minds, emotions, bodies, and how we relate to others. The fall has not just affected us in some ways, but sin has permeated everything about us. We are completely enslaved to sin and have absolutely no moral ability to do good on our own (Romans 3:10-12). It is by the grace of God that anyone, whether a believer or not, does good to his neighbor. This is why Jesus says in John 6:44, "No one can come to me unless the Father who sent me draws him." No human being has the power to come to God in his or her will without the intervention of God Himself. This is also why Jesus stresses the idea of someone needing to be reborn to come into the kingdom of God (John 3:1-8). We must be made completely new. In the same way that we played no part in our physical birth, our spiritual birth is also an act of God.

APPLICATION

Total depravity denounces the idea that man is "basically good." It also shows us that we cannot become good or heal ourselves from our fallen condition. No amount of education, self-help books, government programs, or church participation will solve our problem. God must intervene on our behalf and change our hearts. As we live in the world and interact with people who do not believe in Jesus, we must remember that they are still enslaved to sin. Their fallen nature will influence any behavior or decision they make, so we should not be surprised at the wickedness and evil we see in the world.

Furthermore, we should not expect unbelievers to make decisions that glorify God. And while many unbelievers appear to live seemingly good lives, total depravity tells us that they are spiritually dead. However, we have no reason to place ourselves above them, for we were once the same. Rather, we can respond with compassion. We had no power to change our hearts, but God acted on our behalf and saved us. God has lavished us with the undeserved mercy of God, and we should live in awe that the Lord desired to redeem us in our sin.

ANTHROPOLOGY *Total Depravity*

EFFECTS OF TOTAL DEPRAVITY

MOTIVES
~~Inherently good~~
Selfish & manipulative

PHYSICAL BODIES
~~Perfect~~
Decaying & dying

LOGIC & REASONING
~~Clear & wise~~
Clouded & misguided

RELATIONSHIPS
~~Faithful & trustworthy~~
Prone to struggle

EMOTIONS
~~Reflect God's heart~~
Inconsistent & misplaced

IN THIS SECTION

Incarnation

The Deity of Christ

The Humanity of Christ

Hypostatic Union

Offices of Christ

The Virgin Birth

The Crucifixion

The Resurrection

The Ascension

The Eternal Humanity of Christ

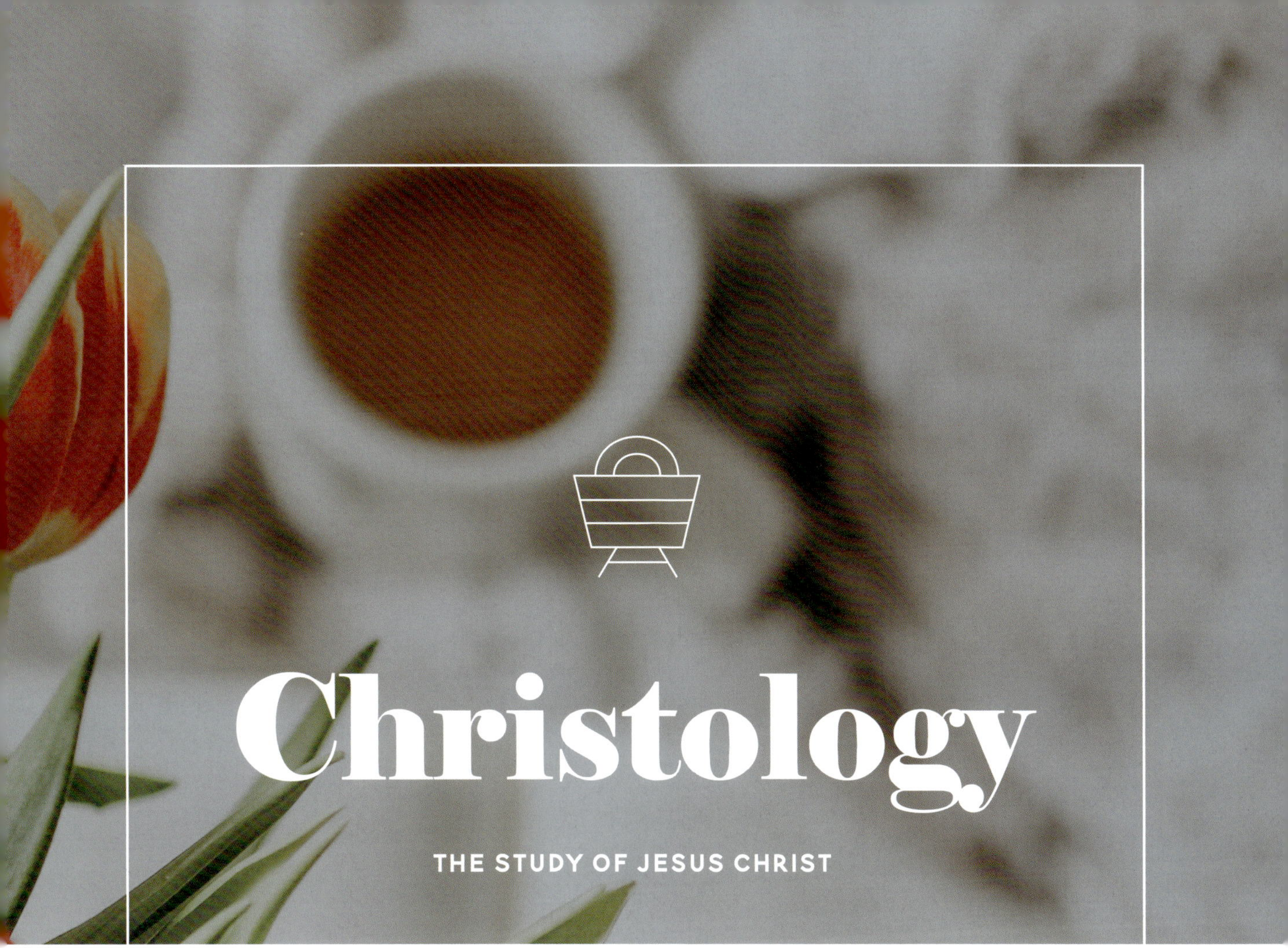

Christology

THE STUDY OF JESUS CHRIST

QUESTIONS ANSWERED

Who is Jesus? | *Is Jesus man or God?* | *What does Jesus do?*

INCARNATION

The incarnation of Christ is His embodiment in the flesh. Before the world was formed, God the Father chose His Son to accomplish His plan of redemption and save His creation from sin. The Son shared glory with the Father in heaven long before the incarnation, but He willingly left His throne and came to earth to redeem us. He remained God, but He laid down His divine privileges for our sake. He became human and was born as a baby, who was named Jesus. The incarnate Son of God revealed the glory of the Father to a weary world. Jesus is the light, grace, and truth of God clothed in humility. Hebrews 10:5 states, "Therefore, as he was coming into the world, he said: You did not desire sacrifice and offering, but you prepared a body for me." The Son of God took on flesh to serve His people and later present this body as a sacrificial offering for their sin. His body would carry sin and receive the punishment for wrongdoing, but Jesus would commit no offense. He was the perfect man, fulfilling God's perfect plan of redemption. Jesus accomplished what only the God-Man could, remaining obedient unto death as He defeated the power of sin and evil.

APPLICATION

John 1:14 says, "The Word became flesh and dwelt among us." The Word is the eternal Son of God, and His incarnation shows that the God of the universe came to us to live like us, though without sin. The incarnate Son of God lived, worked, and rested with His people. Through the Holy Spirit living with us, believers in Christ today still experience this intimate nearness of God, and we know we are never alone.

Just as Christ lived, He also died in the greatest act of sacrificial love the world has ever known. On the cross, Jesus bore the weight of our sins. Though He was blameless in every way, He died so that we could be free. This model of sacrificial love He so perfectly demonstrated in both His life and death serve as an example for us to do the same. Though we will likely never die as He died, we can choose to live as He lived. May we show grace upon grace, think of others before ourselves, help those in need, and show compassion. As we meditate on the mystery of Jesus's incarnation and consider both His life and death, we look forward to His second coming. At that time, Jesus, in His glorified body, will draw near to us once more, bringing His heavenly majesty to earth.

BECAUSE OF CHRIST'S DEITY, *we can know God* THROUGH ALL WE LEARN ABOUT THE LIFE AND WORK OF JESUS IN THE BIBLE.

THE DEITY OF CHRIST

The Deity of Christ means that Jesus is fully God. Christ's deity or divinity is essential to the Christian faith. Colossians 2:9 says, "For the entire fullness of God's nature dwells bodily in Christ," and Philippians 2:6 explains that Jesus came "in the form of God." Hebrews 1:3 says that Jesus is "the exact representation" of God's nature, and Christ's followers attested to the fact that He was God. Peter calls Jesus "the Messiah, the Son of the living God" (Matthew 16:16), and after Jesus's resurrection, Thomas addresses Him, "My Lord and my God!" (John 20:28).

Jesus Himself declared His divinity both explicitly and implicitly. His ability to heal and forgive sins attested to His divine power, as did His ability to raise the dead. Jesus made frequent claims of His oneness with the Father and the authority given to Him by God. John 5:18 states, "he was even calling God his own Father, making himself equal to God." His self-proclaimed identity as Son of Man also spoke to His deity. But perhaps the greatest evidence of His deity is the resurrection. If Christ proclaimed to be all these things but did not rise from the dead, then He could not have been God. However, Jesus did triumph over death; the tomb could not hold Him there. Indeed, He is God.

APPLICATION

Because of Christ's deity, we can know God through all we learn about the life and work of Jesus in the Bible. Jesus explains in John 14:9, "The one who has seen me has seen the Father." Through Jesus, we know the compassion of our God. We know the patience, the strength, the endurance, and the love of our God. We can also find confidence in that because Jesus is God, our sins were forgiven when He died on the cross. If Jesus was not God, He could not have been the perfect sacrifice worthy of atoning for our sins. Not just any man could give His life for our own—the sacrifice required someone wholly spotless, blameless in every way, and this One was the person of Christ. Because Jesus was God in flesh, we can rest in His promises, allowing His perfect authority to govern every part of our lives—what we do, where we go, which words we use, and how we hear and see those around us. We live for Christ alone, for He is God. Indeed, He is worthy of all worship, glory, and praise.

THE HUMANITY OF CHRIST

The humanity of Christ means that while Jesus is fully God, He is also fully man. His humanity is a beautiful but profound and complex reality to grasp. Yet, in taking time to understand Christ's humanity, we understand who He is. While Jesus has eternally existed as God, He took on human flesh during his incarnation. Simply speaking, Jesus was born a human. While the means for His conception are certainly miraculous, His birth was ordinary. He was born as a humble baby and grew as a normal man. Luke 2:52 says that Christ grew "in wisdom and stature, and in favor with God and people." Jesus became like us in every way, except that He never sinned. Jesus had the same physical limitations that we do; He hungered, thirsted, and grew tired. He experienced the strain of temptation, although He did not give into it. He experienced the full range of emotions that we experience in our own lives. He knew anger and trouble in His spirit. He knew tears and desperation. He knew friendship and betrayal. He had blood coursing through his veins. And it would be this very blood that would spill out on our behalf because of who and whose He was.

APPLICATION

If Christ was not human, then He could not be the ultimate sacrifice in our place. Jesus would not have accomplished His work on the cross if He did not become a human. Sacrifice required bloodshed and death. Yet, for salvation to be possible, there needed to be a perfect sacrifice. Christ was fully human yet without sin. His human body with no inkling of sin was necessary to complete the sacrifice on the cross. Hebrews 2:17 says, "Therefore, he had to be like his brothers and sisters in every way…to make atonement for the sins of the people." Christ's humanity also provides Him with the ability to identify with His people. Because Jesus has experienced everything we have, He can identify and sympathize with our pain. We have a God who is able to sympathize with our weaknesses (Hebrews 4:15) and understands and helps us during our temptations since He was also tempted (Hebrews 2:18). When we feel as if we are alone in our suffering, Christ empathizes with us in our pain because He experienced it Himself. When it feels like nobody can understand our grief and our sorrow, Christ understands perfectly. We serve a deeply personal God.

HYPOSTATIC UNION

The hypostatic union of Christ refers to the union of Jesus's human and divine nature in one person. The word "hypostatic" means "personal," so "hypostatic union" is another way of saying "personal union." In the Church's history, some incorrectly taught that Jesus possessed only one of these natures or that He was really two persons living in one body. Essentially, they believed that He would switch on His divine nature and then turn it off and go back to His human nature. However, this idea is not biblical, and it is not affirmed by the Church. Jesus's two natures are completely united. The incarnate Christ was never only human, but He was also never solely divine. He was and is fully man and fully God at the same time.

APPLICATION

The gospel would not exist without the hypostatic union. To save us from our sins, Jesus had to become our perfect substitute and die a human death (Hebrews 2:17). He needed to be completely human to become this substitute, but He also needed to be divine, so He could accomplish what was impossible for every man and woman since the fall of Adam and Eve: a life free from the stain of sin. Because Jesus is fully man, He could take our sin on Himself and pay the penalty of death. Because Jesus is fully God, He can credit His perfect righteousness to us when we trust in Him. And as we draw closer to Him and rely on Him each day to resist sin, He gives us His strength to accomplish what we cannot do on our own. He understands our struggle in His humanity, but He also intercedes for us and gives us His power in His divinity (Hebrews 7:25). He is the fulfillment of all our hearts' needs and longings.

> HE WAS AND IS FULLY MAN AND FULLY GOD AT THE SAME TIME.

FULLY GOD
The Deity of Christ

SYMPATHIZES WITH
OUR WEEKNESS

PAYS OUR PENALTY
OF DEATH

SECURES OUR
RESURRECTION

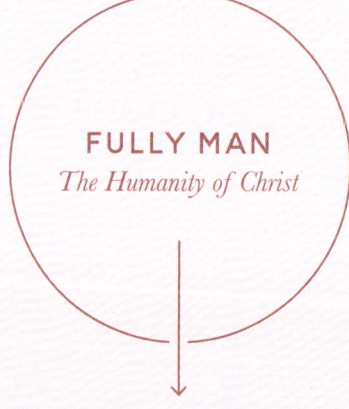

FULLY MAN
The Humanity of Christ

REVEALS
THE FATHER

OUR SINLESS
SACRIFICE

WORTHY
OF WORSHIP

CHRISTOLOGY *Hypostatic Union*

HYPOSTATIC UNION

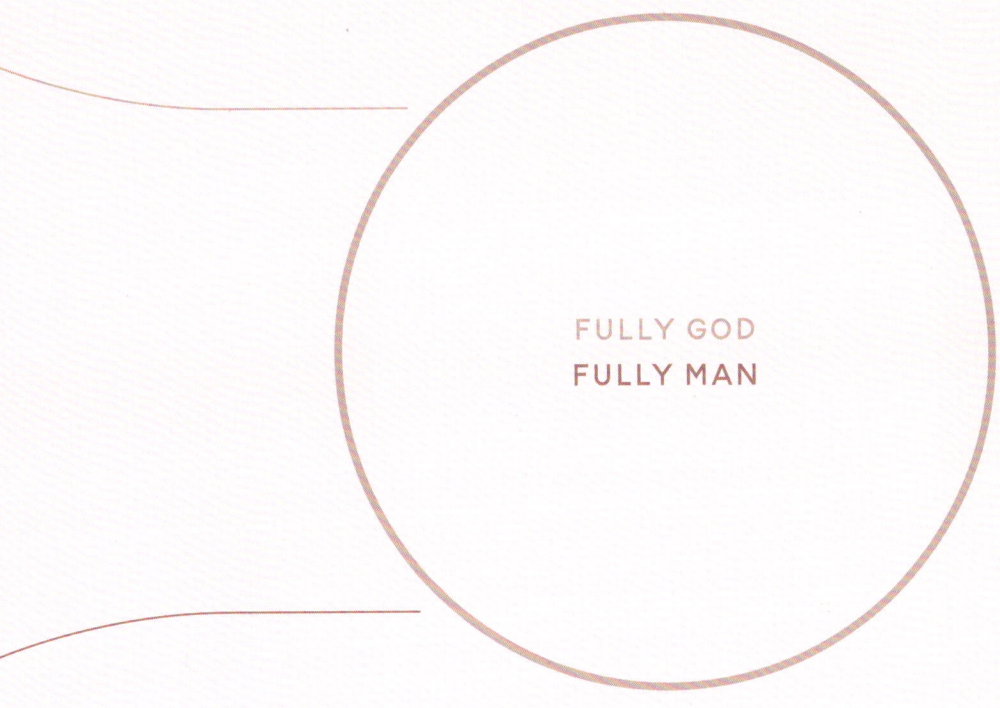

FULLY GOD
FULLY MAN

Because Jesus is fully man, He could take our sin on Himself and pay the penalty of death. | *Because Jesus is fully God, He can credit His perfect righteousness to us when we trust in Him.*

CHRIST IS THE *final and ultimate mediator* WHO HAS RESTORED OUR RELATIONSHIP WITH GOD.

OFFICES OF CHRIST

Prophet, Priest, and King

Christ is the final and ultimate mediator who has restored our relationship with God (1 Timothy 2:5). Because our sin separated us from God, He sent Jesus Christ, His only Son, to the earth. And through His Son's death on the cross, God bridged the gap between Himself and us—a holy God and sinners. However, there were other mediators before Christ who foreshadowed His coming. These mediators fell into three categories or offices: prophets, priests, and kings. Jesus is the ultimate fulfillment of each of these kinds of mediators through His three major offices.

PROPHET

In the Old Testament, prophets acted as spokesmen for the Lord by delivering the words He gave them to the people. Many of the prophets endured suffering and persecution because the people did not like the messages they spoke (Acts 7:52). In the same way, Jesus delivers the Word of God to the people because He is the very Word of God (John 1:14). And just like the prophets before Him, He was rejected and crucified for the message He gave (John 1:11).

PRIEST

Another kind of mediator was a priest. A priest interceded for the people by offering sacrifices to the Lord on their behalf. Jesus is our Great High Priest. Jesus has made intercession for His people by offering Himself as the final, perfect sacrifice for sin. He does not need to offer sacrifices for Himself before going before the Lord because He is sinless. Jesus also does not have to continue to offer sacrifices for us because He was and is the spotless Passover Lamb (Hebrews 7:27). He continues to be the High Priest today at the right hand of God by interceding for His people (Hebrews 12:2).

KING

The final mediator we see in the Old Testament was a king. The Lord gave the kings of Israel their authority, and they were expected to obey the law of the Lord and rule the people in righteousness (1 Kings 2:3). All of the kings of Israel failed to obey the Lord perfectly, but there was one who most resembled the ideal king, although imperfectly. This king was David. The Lord promised David that a King would come from his offspring whose throne would be established forever (2 Samuel 7:8-16). This promise is fulfilled in Christ. Just like David was a shepherd and king, Jesus is our Shepherd King who takes care of His sheep that His Heavenly Father gives Him (John 10:11). Jesus rules the world and will reign forever and ever. His Kingdom "will have no end" (Luke 1:33). We cannot see His Kingdom, even though it is at hand and we are currently a part of it, but we will see it in all of its fullness and splendor when Christ returns.

APPLICATION

Knowing that Jesus fulfills the roles of Prophet, Priest, and King beckons us to rejoice and worship our Savior. All of the Old Testament points to His coming, and all of the New Testament affirms that He is the fulfillment of all things promised in God's Word. Because He is the final Prophet, we can trust His Words because He is the Word made flesh. He spoke what the Father told Him to say because He and the Father are one (John 10:30). Because of this, we can pattern our lives after His words instead of the words of the culture.

Furthermore, because He is the great High Priest, we can trust in His sacrifice on the cross, knowing that He was the perfect Passover Lamb. We do not need to bring Him an offering of rams or goats (Hebrews 10:4), nor do we need to try and earn our salvation through good works. His blood was and is enough. The wrath of God was satisfied in Christ (Romans 5:9). As our Great High Priest, He has given us access into the Holy of Holies—the very presence of God. We can know Him deeply and personally. He is always interceding for us so that we know that our mistakes and failures will not separate us from God. We do not have to work our way to Him.

When we see the broken kingdoms of this world, we can long for Jesus, the true King who is coming, for we belong to an unshakable kingdom where He will forever reign. We need not place our hope in any earthly rulers as we are under Christ's perfect and loving rule now, and we will be part of His physical kingdom forever when He returns.

> **KNOWING THAT JESUS FULFILLS THE ROLES OF PROPHET, PRIEST, AND KING BECKONS US TO REJOICE AND WORSHIP OUR SAVIOR.**

CHRISTOLOGY *Offices of Christ: Prophet, Priest, and King*

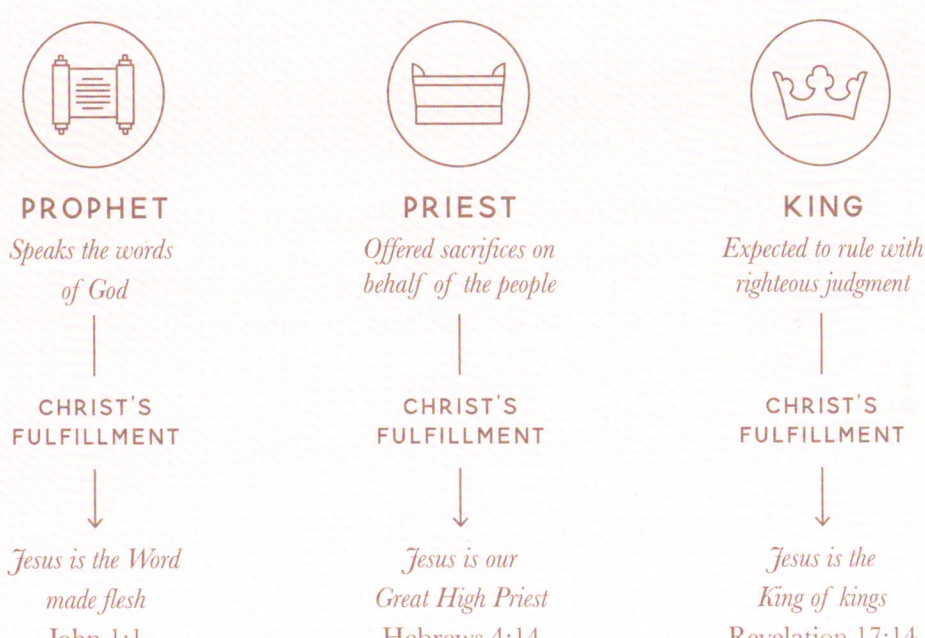

THE VIRGIN BIRTH

The virgin birth, also known as the virginal conception of Jesus, teaches us that Jesus came to earth in the humblest of ways as a baby, born of a woman and conceived through the power of the Holy Spirit (Matthew 1:18). Unlike any birth before or any that would follow, this birth of the promised Messiah was foretold in Isaiah 7:14: "See, the virgin will conceive, have a son, and name him Immanuel."—what a long-awaited prophecy to be fulfilled! And it was fulfilled in Mary, who conceived through God's miraculous intervention. Mary's soon-to-be husband, Joseph, was not involved, nor was any other man (Luke 1:34-35).

APPLICATION

The virgin birth of Christ is one of the assurances that He is the long-awaited and promised Messiah. His divine conception points to His divine nature. As believers, it is His very life, death, and resurrection that is the hope to which we cling. Our righteous King stooped down to become one of us so that through His sacrifice, we, who are so deeply tainted with sin, could one day spend eternity in heaven with Him, standing faultless before His throne and praising Him forevermore.

THE VIRGIN BIRTH OF CHRIST IS ONE OF THE ASSURANCES THAT HE IS THE LONG-AWAITED AND PROMISED MESSIAH.

THE CRUCIFIXION

Jesus experienced the most gruesome form of punishment in His time: crucifixion. In the Roman Empire, crucifixion was considered the most humiliating punishment reserved for the most grievous criminals. Though innocent, Jesus was sentenced to death by the Jews. Before Christ was crucified, He was severely beaten and forced to wear a crown of thorns on His head. During His crucifixion, Jesus was secured to the cross with nails pierced into His feet and hands. His death was slow and torturous as Jesus's position on the cross made it extremely difficult for Jesus to breathe. Laying bare on the cross, Jesus experienced crowds around Him mocking Him and even casting lots for His clothes. He had to listen to people taunt His Lordship saying, "If you are the king of the Jews, save yourself!" (Luke 23:37). Even still, Jesus responded with words of grace. He asked God to forgive those who tortured and taunted Him. After about six hours on the cross, Jesus took His last breath and died.

APPLICATION

Jesus's death on the cross reveals His humanity. If He did not take on human nature, it would have been impossible for Jesus to die. Because He was fully God and fully human, Jesus experienced all of His crucifixion's realities. He felt the pain of the nails in His skin. He felt His body slowly losing life. He felt the struggle of trying to take a breath and having a parched tongue without water. By His great love for us, Jesus willingly took all of this on for our sake. In times of suffering in our own lives, we have a God who knows our pain. We never have to feel like God does not understand our pain, for the cross reveals that He does. He sympathizes with our sufferings, for He too has known suffering.

> WE NEVER HAVE TO FEEL LIKE GOD DOES NOT UNDERSTAND OUR PAIN, FOR THE CROSS REVEALS THAT HE DOES.

THE RESURRECTION

After Jesus was crucified, He was laid to rest in a tomb. However, He did not stay in the tomb, for after three days, Jesus rose from the dead. Jesus's resurrection shows His triumph over sin and death. Jesus is victorious over sin because the powers of sin could not hold Him. Others who saw His physical, risen body also confirmed Jesus's resurrection. His disciples and other witnesses saw Him with their own eyes. They recognized who He was and even touched the nail marks in His hands. Jesus even ate breakfast with His disciples before He ascended. While He was not yet glorified, His physical body demonstrates how His humanity remained after His resurrection. Jesus may have experienced death, but He did not remain dead. He is alive!

APPLICATION

If Jesus remained dead after His crucifixion, there would be no hope for the believer in Christ. There would be no hope for the forgiveness of sins and no hope for life after death. As Paul says in 1 Corinthians 15:14, "if Christ has not been raised, then our proclamation is in vain, and so is your faith." But because Jesus rose from the dead, we know that He holds power over sin and death. Those who trust in Jesus share in His victory. Believers in Christ can triumphantly say that sin does not have a hold on them anymore. They can have confidence knowing that death is not the end for them. Even if they experience death in this life, their salvation with Christ secures for them an eternity with Him forever. Christ's resurrection also shows that there is hope for our future. Jesus's triumph over death means that one day He will rid the world of sin forever. By rising from the grave, Jesus proclaims that death does not have the final word.

BECAUSE JESUS ROSE FROM THE DEAD, WE KNOW THAT HE HOLDS POWER OVER SIN AND DEATH.

THE ASCENSION

The ascension of Christ is an event in the New Testament that we may not often consider, yet it remains an amazing moment in the history of the world and our faith. Jesus's ascension marks the end of His earthly ministry as He defeated sin and death forever through His death on the cross. When Jesus ascended into heaven, He returned to His heavenly home and sits, even now, at the right hand of the Father. As He sits at the Father's right hand, Jesus is enthroned as King. The ascension stands as His coronation ceremony, and He will reign as King forever. Though His kingdom is now unseen, when Jesus rises from His seated position beside the Father, He will return and bring His kingdom to earth. Even though the disciples must have been sorrowful over being separated from Christ, the disciples left the scene of His ascension rejoicing. They witnessed the fulfillment of all of the Old Testament prophecies of the Messianic King from the line of Judah who would reign forever. Jesus may have been physically absent from the world, but His ascension revealed to His disciples where He would be until they met Him again face to face.

APPLICATION

Though we know that Jesus is alive because He has risen and is always present with us, it is hard to be physically separated from Him as we live out our days on earth. However, the ascension gives us comfort in knowing where He is. Jesus is with His Father and sits at His right hand, and there He reigns as King. He will only leave His throne when He brings His kingdom to earth and judges the world. Jesus is also actively working in heaven, and His work involves us! He intercedes for His people by praying for their perseverance. He hears us when we call out to Him, and He understands our sorrows and burdens. Jesus's ascension calls us to look to what is coming—when someday we will go to be with Him. In John 14, Jesus told His disciples that He was going to prepare a place for them. If we dwelt on this promise every day, how different would our lives be? The cares and worries of this world are put in their proper places as we rest in the knowledge that Christ is creating a heavenly home for His people, and we will one day be with Him there.

> **JESUS'S ASCENSION CALLS US TO LOOK TO WHAT IS COMING—WHEN SOMEDAY WE WILL GO TO BE WITH HIM.**

THE LIFE OF CHRIST

VIRGIN BIRTH OF CHRIST

Jesus goes to the temple

| 10 BC | 1 BC | AD 10 |

CHRISTOLOGY *Birth, Crucifixion, Resurrection, Ascension of Christ*

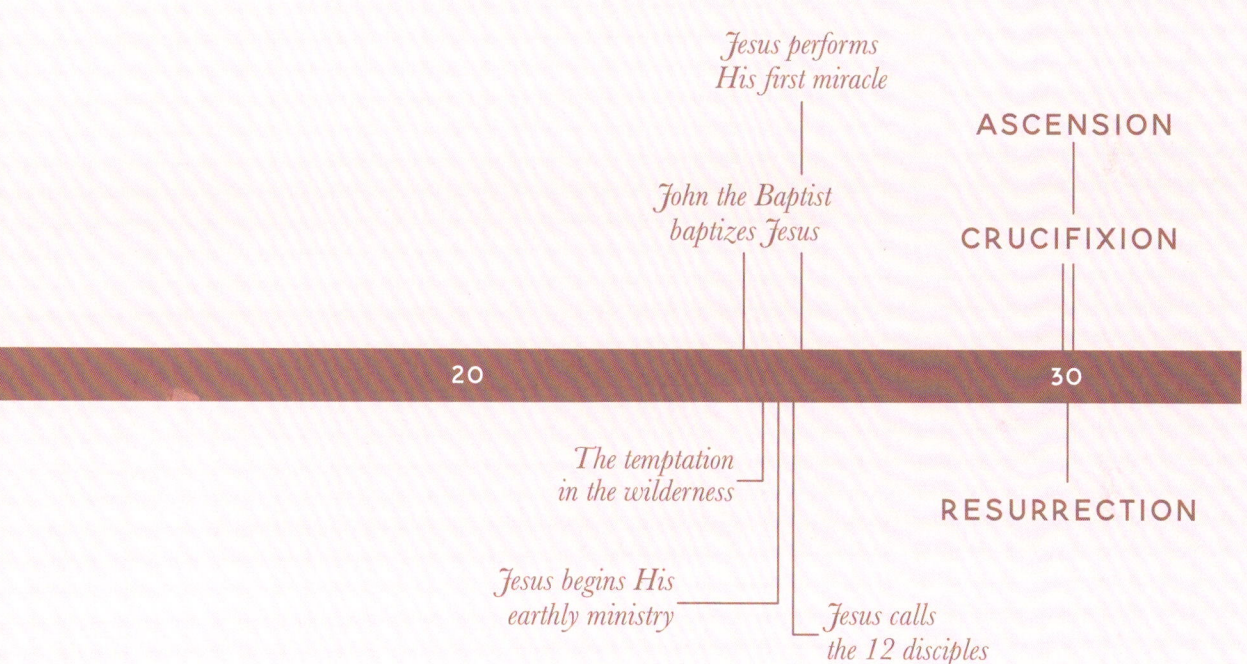

EVIDENCE OF CHRIST'S BODILY RESURRECTION

HE ATE
Luke 24:40-43
↓
Physical hunger

+

THOMAS TOUCHED HIS HANDS & SIDE
John 20:27
↓
Fleshly wounds

HE APPEARED TO MORE THAN 500 PEOPLE AFTER HIS RESURRECTION
1 Corinthians 15:6
↓
Visible presence

THE ETERNAL HUMANITY OF CHRIST

When Jesus came to earth, He humbled Himself from His heavenly position and became human (Philippians 2:7). Jesus's divine status and substance never changed, but when He came to earth, He assumed something that He had not been before. Jesus was born as a baby and took on human nature (Luke 2:7). He lived a human life and died a human death (Luke 2:40, Mark 15:37). When He rose from the dead, Jesus was still human (John 20:27). And when Jesus returned to heaven, He entered the heavenly places and sat at the Father's right hand as a human being. At this very moment, He is still there in heaven, and He is still fully God and fully man. He will forever be both divine and human. This aspect of Christ's nature is very significant. Because Jesus is present in heaven being fully God and fully man, men and women who follow Jesus will enter heaven as human beings because they have been united with Christ. We will one day physically be with God just like Jesus is now (Hebrews 6:20).

APPLICATION

The fact that Jesus still possesses His human nature points to our future bodily resurrection. Jesus's resurrection as a human being demonstrates what will happen to every person who follows Him after they die. Jesus has broken the curse of death, so death will not hold His people forever. Our bodies will be raised from the dead just as Christ's body rose from the grave and ascended into heaven. One day too, we will physically be with the Lord in heaven as He is today (1 Corinthians 15:50-58). Finally, it is important to note that our physical bodies are not bad things to be rid of, but broken things Christ will restore when He returns.

> WE WILL ONE DAY PHYSICALLY BE WITH GOD JUST LIKE JESUS IS NOW.

> IN THIS SECTION

Overview of How to be Saved

Ordo Salutis

Election

Calling

Regeneration

Conversion

Justification

Adoption

Sanctification

Perseverance

Glorification

Union with Christ

Substitutionary Atonement

Double Imputation

Soteriology

THE STUDY OF SALVATION

QUESTIONS ANSWERED

What is salvation? | *What happens after I die?* | *How can I be saved?*

OVERVIEW OF HOW TO BE SAVED

The following section includes the doctrine of salvation, including calling, election, justification, sanctification, and glorification. It is important to reflect on our respective faith. Do you know whether or not you are saved? Are you confident in your standing before a Holy God? Do you know with complete certainty that you are God's child, chosen and loved by Him?

The core of the gospel can be summarized by four categories: creation, fall, redemption, and restoration. In other words, God is good, powerful, and loving, and He created us to be in a relationship with Him (creation). Humankind rejected God and rebelled against Him. Our rebellion not only separates us from God, but it also condemns us to die because the penalty for sin is death (fall). But out of His great love for us, God sent His only Son, Jesus, to save us (redemption). Jesus, who is fully man and fully God, lived a perfect life and died on the cross to pay the penalty for our sins. He rose again three days later and is now seated at the right hand of God. Jesus promises that whoever believes in Him will be forgiven and restored to a right relationship with God. Though now we live by faith, one day, God will return. He will right every wrong, and His children will live forever at peace with Him. This is how He will restore us to Himself.

If you have never placed your trust in Christ, it is not too late. Perhaps you have heard the gospel story before, but it has never seemed relevant to you until now. Or perhaps you believed the gospel as a child but have since doubted your salvation. Or maybe you are walking with the Lord, growing, serving, and involving yourself in the local church. To all, we encourage this simple application: repent and believe. Turn to the finished work of Christ, and rejoice in His beauty and grace. Acknowledge your sin before the Holy God, and submit to His perfection, lordship, and love.

As we surrender our lives to Christ, this looks less like a one-time decision and more like a lifetime covenant. To follow Christ is committing to Him through a promise that you will love, obey, and follow Him wherever He leads. A true Christian is not immune to doubt, nor is any Christian perfect. Though your faith may feel weak at times, remember, it is not a matter of how strong your faith is but in whom you place your trust. Jesus promises that He will never lose any of His sheep, and we can rest in His faithful promises. We have been brought from death to life through belief in the gospel, which is the only hope for our souls. Truly, He will hold us fast.

As you read this section, let these doctrines settle deeply. May the truths of Scripture bring fresh confidence in God's saving power and lead to the repentance, faith, and salvation of many.

THE METANARRATIVE OF SCRIPTURE

CREATION

In the beginning, God created the universe. He made the world and everything in it. He created humans in His own image to be His representatives on the earth.

FALL

The first humans, Adam and Eve, disobeyed God by eating from the fruit of the Tree of Knowledge of Good and Evil. Because of sin, the world was cursed. The punishment for sin is death, and because of Adam's original sin, all humans are sinful and condemned to death.

REDEMPTION

God sent His Son to become a human and redeem His people. Jesus Christ lived a sinless life and died on the cross to pay the penalty for sin. He resurrected from the dead and ascended into heaven. All who put their faith in Jesus are saved from death and freely receive the gift of eternal life.

RESTORATION

One day, Jesus Christ will return again and restore all that sin destroyed. He will usher in a new heaven and new earth where all who trust in Him will live eternally with glorified bodies in the presence of God.

ORDO SALUTIS

The *ordo salutis*, which means "order of salvation," is the sequence of events that make up the process of salvation. Salvation is a work of God from start to finish. The order of salvation is election, calling, regeneration, conversion, justification, adoption, sanctification, perseverance, and glorification. While we often think of salvation as only a one-time event, our salvation has past, present, and future elements. Because our salvation is dependent on God and not upon us, we can be confident that if we are recipients of God's election, He will sustain us as we journey to glorification.

THE ORDER OF SALVATION

1. ELECTION
2. CALLING
3. REGENERATION
4. CONVERSION
5. JUSTIFICATION
6. ADOPTION
7. SANCTIFICATION
8. PERSEVERANCE
9. GLORIFICATION

ELECTION

Election is the act of God choosing whom He will save according to His divine purposes. God's election is a mysterious doctrine. On the one hand, God chose His children before the foundation of the world, and nothing can alter God's plans. He elects whom He wills according to His perfect wisdom (Ephesians 1:4). On the other hand, God grants the opportunity for all to be saved and uses our prayers to accomplish His purposes (Romans 10:1). The doctrine of election resides in this tension. According to His mysterious and divine purposes, God chose some to be ordained to eternal life (1 Thessalonians 1:4-5, Acts 13:48). However, God did not choose us because of anything good or bad we had done (Romans 9:11-13). Without God opening our eyes, none would seek Him (Romans 3:11). He foreknows, predestines, and calls those who will be saved (Romans 8:28-30). God's elect will endure and persevere to the end, and their names are written in the Book of Life (Revelation 13:7-8).

APPLICATION

The doctrine of election should spur us to praise God and share our faith with others. As Christians, we were saved purely according to God's extravagant grace. God did not save us because we were good enough, smart enough, or because we would make a great asset to His team; we were worthy of death and did not deserve to be saved. God's great act of mercy forever changed our lives. If you are a Christian, thank God that He chose you and worked out salvation in your life. Secondly, since we do not know whom God will save, we must share the gospel with anyone and everyone! Some use the idea of election to hinder their evangelistic efforts. Since God has determined who will be saved, they ask, "Why do we need to do anything?" But the truth is, we do not know who God will save, so we must share the gospel with as many people as possible. He wants to use us to share His glory with others, and as Christians, we have been given a global mission to share the gospel to the ends of the earth (Acts 1:8). Our decisions matter; our lives are not fatalistic. Knowing that God will save some should spur us to share the gospel with as many people as possible (2 Timothy 2:10).

ROMANS 8:28

We know that all things work together for the good of those who love God, who are called according to his purpose.

CALLING

Calling refers to the inward drawing of the elect to Jesus Christ. The elect are the people who were divinely appointed to salvation by God. In eternity past, God selected those whom He would save from sin and reconcile to Himself. Then, God appointed particular moments in time to carry these chosen individuals out of their state of death and rebellion. At these times, the elect are freed from their sinful nature and brought into life in Jesus Christ. How does the calling within believers work? By His grace, God enlightens the lost chosen to His Word and plan of salvation. He leads them to repentance and softens their heart. He blesses them with Spirit-generated faith in Jesus Christ. He gives them the desire to please Him and the ability to do so. As a result, this type of calling is effectual. Whereas general calling is the message of the gospel that goes out indiscriminately to all people, effectual calling means that the particular people who receive the inward work of the Holy Spirit will indeed freely and willingly come to Jesus Christ by God's grace.

APPLICATION

Like election, calling is based on the power and work of God. 2 Timothy 1:9 says, "He has saved us and called us with a holy calling, not according to our works, but according to his own purpose and grace, which was given to us in Christ Jesus before time began." When we hear the gospel, we do not possess any moral ability to respond on our own. We are hard-hearted and dead in sin. But, the Holy Spirit makes us alive through the gift of faith so that when we receive God's revelation, we want to cling to the salvation of Jesus. This truth makes us humble and grateful to the Lord for calling us to Himself.

Furthermore, the doctrine of calling motivates believers to present the gospel message to all. Calling is wholly the work of the Spirit, but at the same time, God uses people to seek the lost and tell them of His love. Your evangelism will open the door for the sinner to believe, and God might use your commitment to his or her salvation to draw them to Christ.

GENERAL CALLING	EFFECTUAL CALLING
EXTERNAL	INTERNAL
GOES OUT TO ALL PEOPLE	GOES OUT TO THE ELECT
CAN BE REJECTED	RESULTS IN CONVERSION

REGENERATION

Regeneration refers to the transformation that a believer undergoes when he or she comes to faith in Christ. 2 Corinthians 5:17 says, "Therefore, if anyone is in Christ, he is a new creation; the old has passed away, and see, the new has come!" The word "regeneration" means "rebirth," and God's hands accomplish this act of transformation as He removes sin from our lives and washes us anew. Before coming to know Christ, our hearts are sinful and in desperate need of renewal. When we experience the saving work of Christ, we receive a heart transplant of sorts. The sinful heart is removed as a new, holy one takes its place. Ezekiel 11:19-20 explains this process by saying, "I will give them integrity of heart and put a new spirit within them; I will remove their heart of stone from their bodies and give them a heart of flesh, so that they will follow my statutes, keep my ordinances, and practice them. They will be my people, and I will be their God." Christ's grace and mercy give us renewal. We were once dead in our sins, but in His grace, He has made us alive in Him. By Him, we are born again and completely transformed.

APPLICATION

Regeneration not only changes our hearts, but it reorients our desires. A sinful heart will only have desires to gratify the flesh, but a renewed heart will have desires to glorify the Lord. Over time, those who come to faith in Christ should notice a shift in their motivations, actions, and attitudes. But while these pursuits are present, dying to sin is still very much a reality. Daily we must continue to put off the sinful ways of our old selves and put on the holy ways of our new selves in Christ (Colossians 3:5-10). We may still find it difficult to die to ourselves, but we can find encouragement in that God has given us a new heart. In effect, we can fight our sin and pursue godliness because of it.

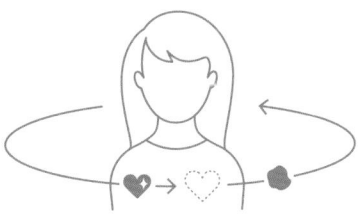

EZEKIEL 36:26

I will give you a new heart and put a new spirit within you;
I will remove your heart of stone and give you a heart of flesh.

CONVERSION

Conversion is the act of repenting from sin and turning to Christ in faith. On our own, all humans are walking in sin. When conversion occurs, God's call of salvation changes the convert from walking in sin to walking in faith in Christ. Both repentance and faith are necessary and work together to complete conversion. When God opens our eyes to see the gravity of our sin, we are aware of our desperate need for Christ. This awareness causes us to confess our sin and turn away from it to follow Jesus. Repentance is not only grief over sin but a desire to abandon it altogether. Our faith in Christ comes from a belief in the person of Jesus and the work of the gospel. When we repent from our sins, we understand that it is only by the cross of Christ that we receive forgiveness and salvation. Romans 10:9 says, "If you confess with your mouth, 'Jesus is Lord,' and believe in your heart that God raised him from the dead, you will be saved." God saves those who have faith in Christ and repent of their sins.

APPLICATION

The call to follow Christ is not one to say a prayer to be saved from hell, but rather, it involves a life change—a heart change. God's calling to follow Him is an invitation for us to turn away from our old ways. While entering into a personal relationship with the Lord does not mean we will never mess up, it does mean that our greatest desire becomes to glorify the Lord in all that we say and do. True faith surely changes us as we become more like Christ through the Lord's calling to follow Him.

CONVERT | *epistrephō* | To turn

JUSTIFICATION

Justification is an act of God in which He declares a person righteous or just. In light of God's character, we have to answer a fundamental question: How can an unjust person stand before the final judgment of a just and holy God? In Psalm 130:3, David gives us the answer: "Lord if you kept account of iniquities, Lord, who could stand?" No human being can stand before the Lord and live because we are sinful and God is holy (Exodus 33:20). To be in the presence of God, we need to be justified, and we cannot justify ourselves. Justification is one of the central doctrines of the Christian faith. It is rooted in the very heart of the gospel and reveals to believers how we are redeemed. God justifies us—or declares us to be righteous—because when we are given a new heart by the Lord and faith from Him to believe in Jesus as our Savior, we are united with Christ and take on His righteousness. This righteousness is positional righteousness, a legal standing before God. Christ dealt with our sinfulness on the cross as He bore the wrath of God and took our sins on Himself. We can stand before God because when He looks upon us, He sees the righteousness of His Son.

APPLICATION

The doctrine of justification means that we can put an end to our striving to earn our way to heaven or gain God's approval. We can walk in the freedom that comes from knowing that our standing before God does not depend on anything that we can do or be on our own. Our standing depends completely on who Jesus is and what He has done. We are perfectly righteous in the eyes of God—even though we still struggle with sin—because God does not base our righteousness on our works but the finished work of Christ. Our justification does not mean that we become lazy toward our spiritual growth. On the contrary, the doctrine of justification grows our love and affection for the Lord and how He has worked on our behalf. Effectually, we pursue righteous living out of our confidence in knowing that we are united with Christ and can never be separated from Him.

VERDICT: *Not guilty*

WHEN THE LORD *regenerates* OUR HEARTS AND *justifies* US, WE ARE *adopted* AS HIS SONS AND DAUGHTERS.

ADOPTION

Adoption is the process by which God makes us His children and brings us into His family. When Jesus was completing His earthly ministry, it would have been very uncommon to call the Lord "Father." However, almost every recorded prayer of Jesus includes His address of the Lord as His Father. What is even more astounding is that when Jesus instructs His disciples how to pray, He tells them to do the same (Matthew 6:9-13), displaying one of the most beautiful truths about the gospel. When the Lord regenerates our hearts and justifies us, we are adopted as His sons and daughters. He does not just rid us of sin and leave us; He takes us in and calls us His own. He puts His name on us. Ephesians 1 tells us that God predestined His chosen people for adoption as sons and daughters before the very foundation of the world. As soon as Adam and Eve rebelled against Him, God put His plan of adoption into motion. He was going to bring back His children.

APPLICATION

Because of the gospel and our adoption into the family of God, our entire identity changes. We are new creations in Christ, and we no longer belong to the domain of darkness but the kingdom of Jesus (Colossians 1:13). This means that the Lord is our Father, and we are now His children. We have access to our Father, and He delights in us. When we are fearful or wrestling with sin, we can call out to the Lord as a child cries for his mother or father, and He hears us (Romans 8:15). He will help us. He is the only Father we have who is completely perfect and good. Our adoption has also made us a co-heir with Christ (Romans 8:16). We are united with Jesus through His righteousness. And, Jesus has placed His righteousness upon us so that God can adopt us. We have access to the blessings and treasures that belong to Him. Nothing on this earth could ever replace or compare to the riches and joy of being a co-heir with Christ. This also means that as we fellowship with other believers, we stand alongside fellow co-heirs, and we will one day reunite in the presence of the Lord. The body of Christ is our true family, and the kingdom of God our true home.

SANCTIFICATION

Sanctification is the progressive work of God in our lives to grow us in Christlikeness. God declares us positionally righteous through justification. Then, He makes us righteous through the process of sanctification. In sanctification, we become who we really are in Christ. To be sanctified is to be purified as we increasingly walk in obedience to God's commands. Sanctification begins at the moment we are saved and continues through the rest of our lives. As we actively grow in holiness through His Word and increasingly put off sinful thoughts, desires, and actions, we grow to look more like our Savior. Although there will certainly be times we will fall back into our sinful ways, if we are walking with Christ, we will increasingly turn from those ways and to our Father instead, whose Spirit lives within us. However, we will only be fully sanctified and free from sin when we finally see God face to face.

APPLICATION

If we are in Christ, we should pursue the things of God with our entire beings—heart, soul, mind, and strength. Growing in personal holiness will not save us, nor will God love us more based on our growth. He is perfectly satisfied with us and loves us deeply, regardless of what we do. Our obedience to God is not to earn His favor but because of love for Him. Our obedience is for His glory and our good. It is important to remember that our growth in sanctification is not based on how we feel. As we grow in sanctification, our knowledge of God's holiness and our depravity will surely grow. We may even feel like greater sinners than we were before we were saved. But when we love Christ and honor Him with our lives, we will grow in true holiness in our thoughts, actions, and behaviors as evidence of the Spirit's work in our lives. When we love Christ, we desire to please Him by saying no to sin and obeying His commands.

> IN SANCTIFICATION, WE BECOME
> WHO WE REALLY ARE IN CHRIST.

SOTERIOLOGY *Ordo Salutis: Sanctification*

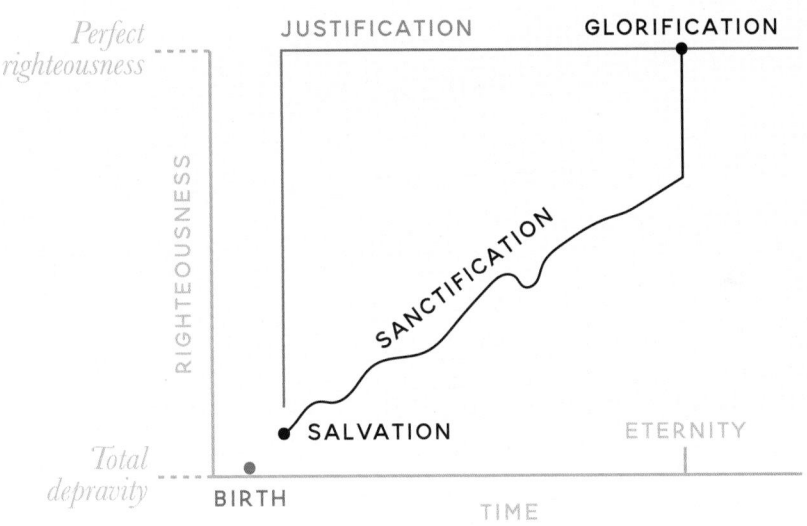

PERSEVERANCE

Perseverance means that all who find salvation in Jesus Christ will be kept by God's saving grace and will persevere as Christians until the end of their lives. God's work to cause believers to persevere means that those who are truly saved cannot lose their salvation. John 10:27-29 says, "My sheep hear my voice, I know them, and they follow me. I give them eternal life, and they will never perish. No one will snatch them out of my hand. My Father, who has given them to me, is greater than all. No one is able to snatch them out of the Father's hand." As Christians persevere through life, trials will certainly come, but no trial will be great enough to remove them from God's hand. Though believers may sometimes waver for a moment, questioning their desire to persevere through hardships and trials, lifelong faith in Jesus Christ is evidence of genuine and true salvation. Hebrews 3:14 says, "For we have become participants if we hold firmly until the end the reality that we had at the start."

APPLICATION

Perseverance is a great comfort to believers as we navigate the trials and temptations of this life. When we face difficult circumstances that threaten to crush us, we can be confident that it is God's power that sustains our faith. When we wrestle with questions and doubts, we can rest assured that the Lord is guarding and upholding us. When we battle sin in our hearts, we can take comfort knowing that our salvation does not depend on us but on Him. He will complete the good work that He began in us (Philippians 1:6). The doctrine of perseverance points us to hope in the promise of Christ—that He will bring His work in us to completion when we breathe our last, and we will forever stand with Him in victory.

JOHN 10:27-28

My sheep hear my voice, I know them, and they follow me.
I give them eternal life, and they will never perish.
No one will snatch them out of my hand.

SOTERIOLOGY *Ordo Salutis: Perseverance, Glorification*

GLORIFICATION

Glorification is the last step in the order of salvation. Glorification is the complete and final removal of sin when Christ returns—when believers will no longer have earthly bodies but new bodies (1 Corinthians 15:42-44)—raised, changed, and made like Christ's. After His death on the cross, Jesus was the first to rise with His glorified body, and on the day when the final trumpet sounds (1 Corinthians 15:52), we too will be raised up in glory (Romans 8:11). Philippians 3:20-21 reminds us, "our citizenship is in heaven, and we eagerly wait for a Savior from there, the Lord Jesus Christ. He will transform the body of our humble condition into the likeness of his glorious body." At the very moment our glorification takes place, sin will be no more. And we will reign with Christ in the new heaven and earth and experience perfect joy in the Lord's presence as we glorify Him for eternity.

APPLICATION

As we look forward to the day when we shed our physical, earthly bodies for an eternal one with Christ, He offers us hope—hope in knowing that our present struggles are nothing compared to the glory that is to be revealed on the day of Christ Jesus (Romans 8:18). Our suffering is temporary, and it is in that suffering, and even in our greatest joys, that we cling to the hope of Christ. When He returns and raises us to be with Him, all will be made right—sin will vanquish, and there will be no more death, pain, or sadness (Revelation 21:4). We can look upon the scars from life's challenges as beautiful marks of sanctification—marks gained as we faced the hard places in life, pressing into Jesus, growing our faith and love for Him, knowing He would not leave us there. We remember that this world with its brokenness is fleeting, so we cling to what is everlasting—eternity with Jesus.

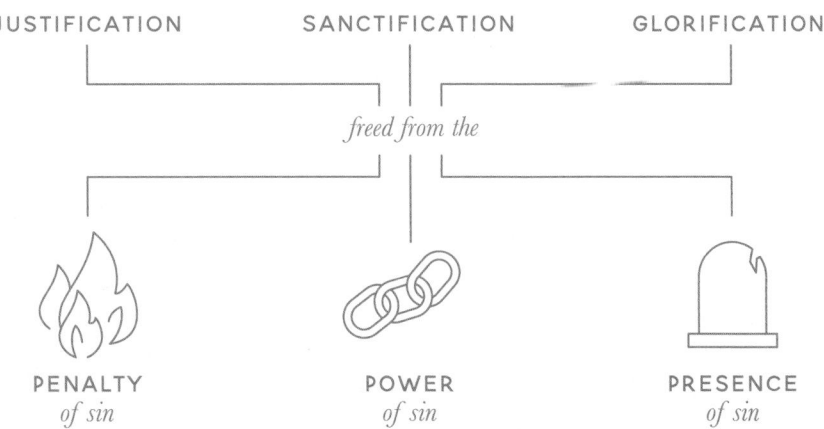

OUR IDENTITY

APART FROM CHRIST	IN CHRIST
Sinners	Saints
Recipients of God's wrath	Recipients of God's grace
Condemned	Free from condemnation
Dead in our sin	Dead to sin
Slaves to sin	Redeemed
Enemies of God	New Creations
Haters of God	Members of the body of Christ
Sons of disobedience	Sons of God
Children of wrath	Co-heirs with Christ
	Sanctified
	Justified
	Glorified
	Eternally alive

UNION WITH CHRIST

Union with Christ is the way by which Jesus's life, death, and resurrection transform our lives. When we put our faith in Jesus Christ for salvation, we are united to Him. Union with Christ means that Christ is in us, and we are in Christ. When we are united to Christ, He is our representative, and what is true of Him is true of us. Jesus's righteousness becomes our righteousness. When Jesus died on the cross to pay for our sins, we died to sin with Him. When Jesus rose from the grave, followers of Christ were raised to new spiritual life with Him and will one day be physically resurrected like Him as well. The Holy Spirit makes sinners, who were dead in sin, alive in Christ by awakening their hearts to the gospel and moving them to cling to the work of Jesus.

APPLICATION

If we are united to Christ through faith, what is true of Jesus is true of us. That means that our value, worth, and identity are not tied up in what we have done but in what Christ has done. We don't have to carry the shame of our sins and mistakes because we have been given the righteousness of Jesus. We don't have to be good enough because Jesus is good enough. We belong to Him, and He is ours. Our union with Christ also means we have the power of Christ to turn away from our sin and walk in obedience. When we are weak, we have His strength. This bond is unshakeable. Because we have union with Christ, we can trust in Romans 8:39, which states that "height nor depth, nor any other created thing will be able to separate us from the love of God that is in Christ Jesus our Lord." Nothing can remove us from the hands of the one who made us and who called us to Himself.

>WHEN WE PUT OUR FAITH IN JESUS CHRIST FOR SALVATION, WE ARE UNITED TO HIM.

SUBSTITUTIONARY ATONEMENT

Substitutionary atonement describes the act of Jesus Christ taking the punishment for sin and dying in place of sinners. "To atone" means to make reparations for an offense. Scripture makes clear that all people are rebellious and corrupt. Instead of worshiping the true, holy, and loving God, all have forsaken Him to follow their own desires. For this reason, all people deserve death and eternal separation from God. Steeped in sin, we have no moral capacity to atone for the crimes we have committed against God, our Creator. But, because God is merciful and compassionate, He provided a way for sinners to be reconciled to Himself. God restored our relationship with Him through the substitutionary atonement of Jesus Christ. Jesus died on the cross as our substitute to make atonement for our sins.

In the Old Testament, God instituted a worship system of sacrifice that pointed to the ultimate saving work of Christ. The ancient Israelites usually sacrificed a spotless lamb to pay for their sin. Through this act, they exercised faith in the sacrifice of God's chosen Savior to come. Jesus was this perfect sacrificial Lamb. As the sinless and obedient Son, He stood in our place before the wrath of God. Though He was innocent of all crimes, Jesus took on our sins. He was led like a sheep to the slaughter. Suffering whips, beatings, and crucifixion, Jesus underwent a gruesome criminal's death. Isaiah 53:5 says, "he was pierced because of our rebellion, crushed because of our iniquities; punishment for our peace was on him, and we are healed by his wounds." Jesus's death on the cross was the true substitutionary atonement. And, through His payment, Jesus satisfied the justice of God and brought us into the love of the Father.

APPLICATION

Through Christ's substitutionary atonement for our sins, Christians are freed of guilt and shame. Jesus's blood that was spilled on the cross covered us completely so that when He looks at us, He no longer sees our sin but the righteousness of His Son. He has forgiven us of our debt, and in the same way, we can extend forgiveness to those who wrong us. Without the sacrifice of Jesus, we could never know this kind of forgiveness. Though there are certainly times when we would rather hold on to bitterness toward another, we remember that Jesus gave His life so that we could be granted forgiveness for our shortcomings. In humble confession, we come to the Lord broken over our sin yet rejoicing because Christ took our place. And because He took our place, we have been given access to the Father — access to "approach the throne of grace with boldness, so that we may receive mercy and find grace to help us in time of need" (Hebrews 4:16).

SOTERIOLOGY *Substitutionary Atonement*

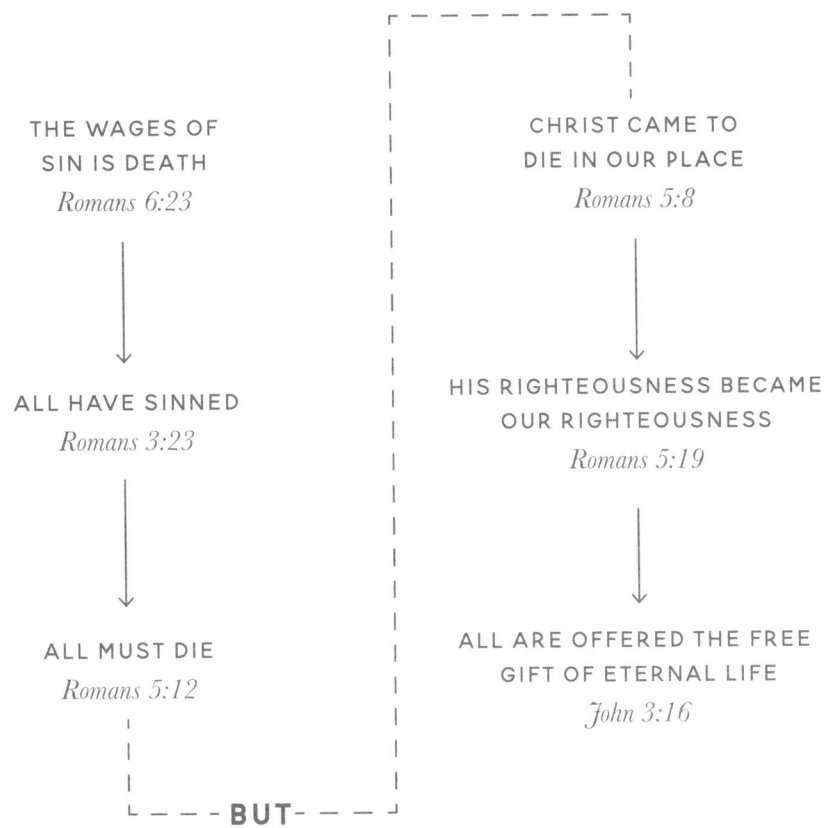

AS WE LIVE THE CHRISTIAN LIFE, WE *rest* IN THIS RIGHTEOUSNESS AND *live out* THIS RIGHTEOUSNESS.

DOUBLE IMPUTATION

Through Christ's work of justification, those who trust in Him are declared righteous. However, believers are only declared righteous through the imputation of Christ's righteousness to us. The word "imputation" describes a transference—when something is attributed to something or someone else. Through Jesus's sacrifice, our sin is imputed to Christ, and His righteousness is imputed to us. In other words, He takes on our sin, pays its penalty on the cross, and gives us His perfect righteousness. This act is referred to as double imputation or the "great exchange." 2 Corinthians 5:21 says, "He made the one who did not know sin to be sin for us, so that in him we might become the righteousness of God."

APPLICATION

Double imputation is a one-time act that remains constant for believers. Those who trust in Jesus are declared righteous for the remainder of their lives. In times of doubting whether God has truly forgiven our sins, we can remember Christ's perfect righteousness that has been given to us. In the eyes of God, we are more than not guilty of our sins; we are righteous people. As we live the Christian life, we rest in this righteousness and live out this righteousness. Paul writes in Romans 6:13, "And do not offer any parts of [your body] to sin as weapons for unrighteousness. But as those who are alive from the dead, offer yourselves to God, and all the parts of yourselves to God as weapons for righteousness." As believers, we live as instruments of righteousness by dying to sin that once ruled us and living holy and blameless lives for the sake of Christ.

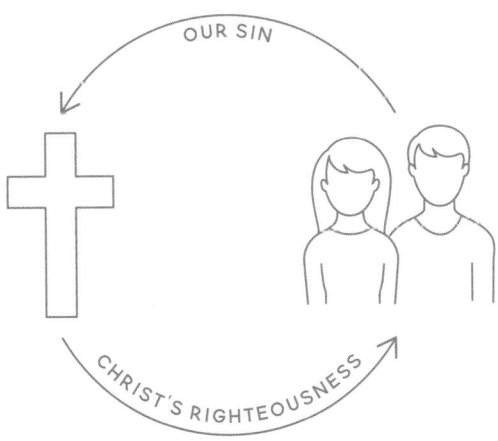

IN THIS SECTION

Personhood of the Holy Spirit

Indwelling of the Holy Spirit

Fruit of the Spirit

Spiritual Gifts

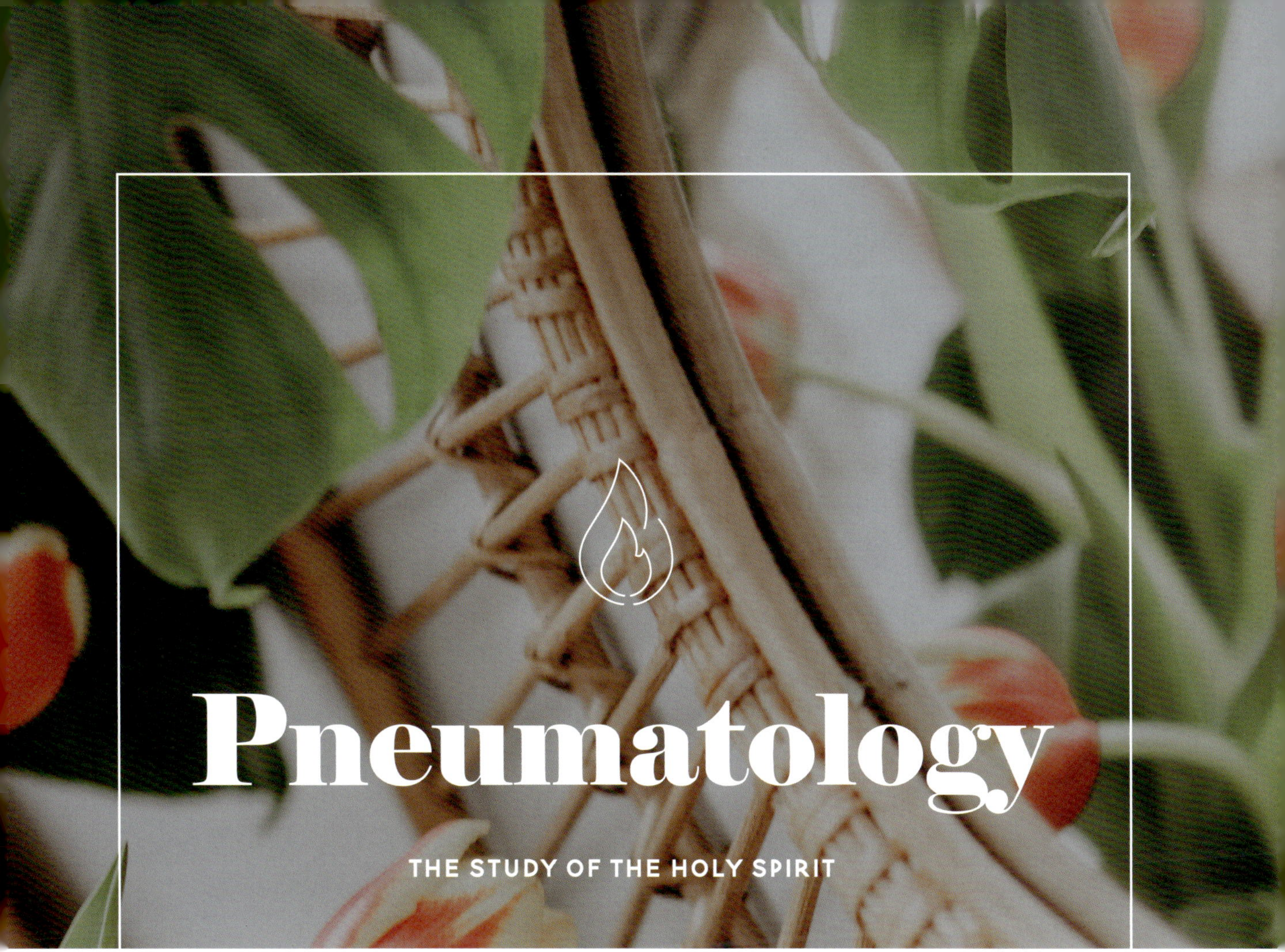

Pneumatology

THE STUDY OF THE HOLY SPIRIT

QUESTIONS ANSWERED

Who is the Holy Spirit? | What does the Holy Spirit do? | Does the Holy Spirit matter for my life?

PERSONHOOD OF THE HOLY SPIRIT

The Holy Spirit is a distinct person of the Trinity and is fully God. His personhood is evidenced through His characteristics and actions in Scripture. The Spirit has always existed and was with the Father at the beginning of creation. He plays an essential role in our salvation by convicting us of sin (John 16:8), which in turn leads us to repent and believe in Jesus. The Holy Spirit strengthens and equips us for the good works that God has prepared for us to do. He gives us life and sustains us (Romans 8:6), purifying, unifying, guiding, and directing us. He is our comforter, helping us in our weaknesses. He provides assurance and evidence of God's presence and reveals the Father's love to us. He teaches and illuminates God's Word as we study and meditate on Scripture. Before His crucifixion, Jesus said that it was better that He leave us so that we could have the Spirit here (John 16:7). And indeed, when we trust in Jesus, the Spirit of God comes and lives within us, guiding us until the end of our lives here on earth.

APPLICATION

Though fully God, the Spirit can sometimes remain the most neglected member of the Trinity. We know that He is important and that He is always near, but we do not know what He does or how to engage with Him. As we learn about the Holy Spirit through Scripture, we can recognize His work in our lives. When we feel the comfort of God's presence or understand a verse in Scripture, it is the work of the Spirit in our lives. When we feel conviction for a harsh word or unwise decision, it is the Spirit's work in our lives. And when we continue to sin after being convicted, we grieve the Spirit. As Christians, we must aim to be sensitive to the Spirit's leading, praying to God for His help, wisdom, comfort, and grace in our lives through the power of His Spirit in us.

THE HOLY SPIRIT IS A DISTINCT PERSON OF THE TRINITY AND IS FULLY GOD.

INDWELLING OF THE HOLY SPIRIT

When we come to faith in Jesus Christ, God gives us the Holy Spirit to dwell within us. When Jesus came, He promised that the Holy Spirit would remain with God's people and live inside them (John 14:17). This residence gives us a permanent union with Jesus since He and the Holy Spirit are one. Romans 8:9-10 states, "You, however, are not in the flesh, but in the Spirit if indeed the Spirit of God lives in you. If anyone does not have the Spirit of Christ, he does not belong to him. Now if Christ is in you, the body is dead because of sin, but the Spirit gives life because of righteousness." Through the indwelling Holy Spirit, we have an intimate relationship with Jesus Himself. The Holy Spirit softens our hearts and generates our faith in Christ. By applying the saving work of Jesus to our lives, He renovates us by transforming our inner being. We are no longer dead in sin or slaves to its power, but our souls have been set free and made alive in Christ. We become living temples for God's glory (1 Corinthians 6:19-20). Scripture also says that the indwelling Holy Spirit is the sign of our adoption into the family of God (Romans 8:15-17) and our guaranteed inheritance of eternal life (Ephesians 1:13-14).

APPLICATION

With the Holy Spirit dwelling in us, we know that God is with us always. We navigate the hardships of this world with the Great Counselor and Comforter. When we feel alone, abandoned, or have been hurt or disappointed, the Holy Spirit reminds us that we are God's beloved children. When we need direction, He helps us correctly interpret and apply Scripture. When we are weak, He leads us to lay our burdens down in prayer. To the Father, He brings the longings of our hearts which we cannot put into words (Romans 8:26). We still live in a fallen world and wrestle with our old ways, but the Holy Spirit convicts us of persistent sins and progressively cultivates us into the image of Christ. As we pursue loving and obeying God, the Holy Spirit molds us into who we were meant to be. Finally, the Holy Spirit empowers us for ministry. Believers are given specific gifts to glorify God and lead others to Jesus. We can ask the Holy Spirit to help us boldly proclaim the gospel and invite Him to stir passion in our hearts for a life of worship.

ROLES OF THE HOLY SPIRIT

CONVICTS US
OF SIN

STRENGTHENS
& EQUIPS US

DOES THE WORK
OF REGENERATION

GIVES US LIFE
& SUSTAINS US

PURIFIES, UNIFIES,
GUIDES, & DIRECTS US

COMFORTS
US

GIVES ASSURANCE
& EVIDENCE OF
GOD'S PRESENCE

REVEALS THE
FATHER'S LOVE
TO US

TEACHES &
ILLUMINATES GOD'S
WORD TO US

INDWELLING OF THE HOLY SPIRIT

FAITH IN CHRIST → *The Holy Spirit living within us*

> AS WE LEARN ABOUT THE HOLY SPIRIT THROUGH SCRIPTURE, WE CAN *recognize His work in our lives.*

THE FRUIT OF THE SPIRIT

LOVE
1 Corinthians 13:1

GOODNESS
Romans 12:9

JOY
John 15:11

FAITHFULNESS
Hebrews 11:1

PEACE
Colossians 3:15

GENTLENESS
James 3:17

PATIENCE
Ephesians 4:2

SELF-CONTROL
1 Corinthians 9:25

KINDNESS
Ephesians 4:32

FRUIT OF THE SPIRIT

The Greek word translated to be "fruit" refers to the natural product of a living thing. Paul uses the term "fruit" when referencing the Holy Spirit at work in every believer to produce "love, joy, peace, patience, kindness, goodness, faithfulness, gentleness and self-control" (Galatians 5:22-23). These nine characteristics are produced by the Holy Spirit, not the individual believer. God gives those who receive salvation through Jesus Christ the Holy Spirit's help to guide them and shape them into the likeness of Jesus. Just as fruit needs time to grow and ripen, so the fruit of the Spirit is cultivated in the lives of Christians as they mature and grow in their faith. Through obedience and faithfulness, the believer will see evidence as the Spirit produces the fruit of love, joy, peace, patience, kindness, goodness, faithfulness, gentleness, and self-control in their own lives.

APPLICATION

As the Holy Spirit is faithful to work in our lives, He works in and through us in a way that causes us to reflect more and more of Christ (2 Corinthians 3:17-18). God's desire for His children is for them to grow into the likeness of Christ so that they are conformed to His image. He has given us His Holy Spirit to help us, intercede for us, shape us, and strengthen us as we grow to be more loving, more joy-filled, more peace-minded, more patient, more kind, more full of goodness, more faithful, more gentle, and more self-controlled. And when we come face to face with the Lord one day in eternity, we will be like Him, perfectly representing the fruit of the Spirit.

2 CORINTHIANS 3:18

We all, with unveiled faces, are looking as in a mirror at the glory of the Lord and are being transformed into the same image from glory to glory; this is from the Lord who is the Spirit.

SPIRITUAL GIFTS

When we come to faith in Christ, the Holy Spirit gives us spiritual gifts. These gifts vary from person to person. Examples from Scripture include teaching, service, healing, wisdom, and prophecy. Some of these gifts are in line with natural abilities, while others are considered miraculous gifts. The purpose of the spiritual gifts is for the edification of the Church. Gifts are not to benefit individual believers but the body of Christ as a whole. Because these gifts are not for ourselves, we should understand that we do nothing to earn them; they are given to us by the Spirit. The Spirit also chooses to give gifts as He so wills (1 Corinthians 12:11). Each one is essential to the body of Christ, and as no one gift is greater than the other, there are no grounds for boasting in them. Believers should desire to live out their unique gifts, not being envious of others but celebrating their own gifts and using them to serve the Church. When all believers are actively using their gifts as God designed, the body of Christ is united and built up to glorify the Lord.

APPLICATION

We should not ignore our Spiritual gifts but seek to identify them and actively use them. While some spiritual tests are helpful to determine our gifts, the best way to gain insight into our gifts is to ask God to reveal them to us and ask others to explain the gifts they see in us. We should also keep feelings of inadequacy from causing us not to use our gifts. Even though we know that each person's gift is different, we can still sometimes feel as though our gifts pale in comparison to others; we may feel as though we are not fit for the specific gift the Holy Spirit has given us. Yet, because the Spirit intentionally blesses us with our gifts, He is the one who empowers us to use them. We should be excited to use these gifts, knowing that it helps equip the Church to look more like Christ.

1 CORINTHIANS 12:12

For just as the body is one and has many parts, and all the parts of that body, though many, are one body — so also is Christ.

PNEUMATOLOGY *Spritual Gifts*

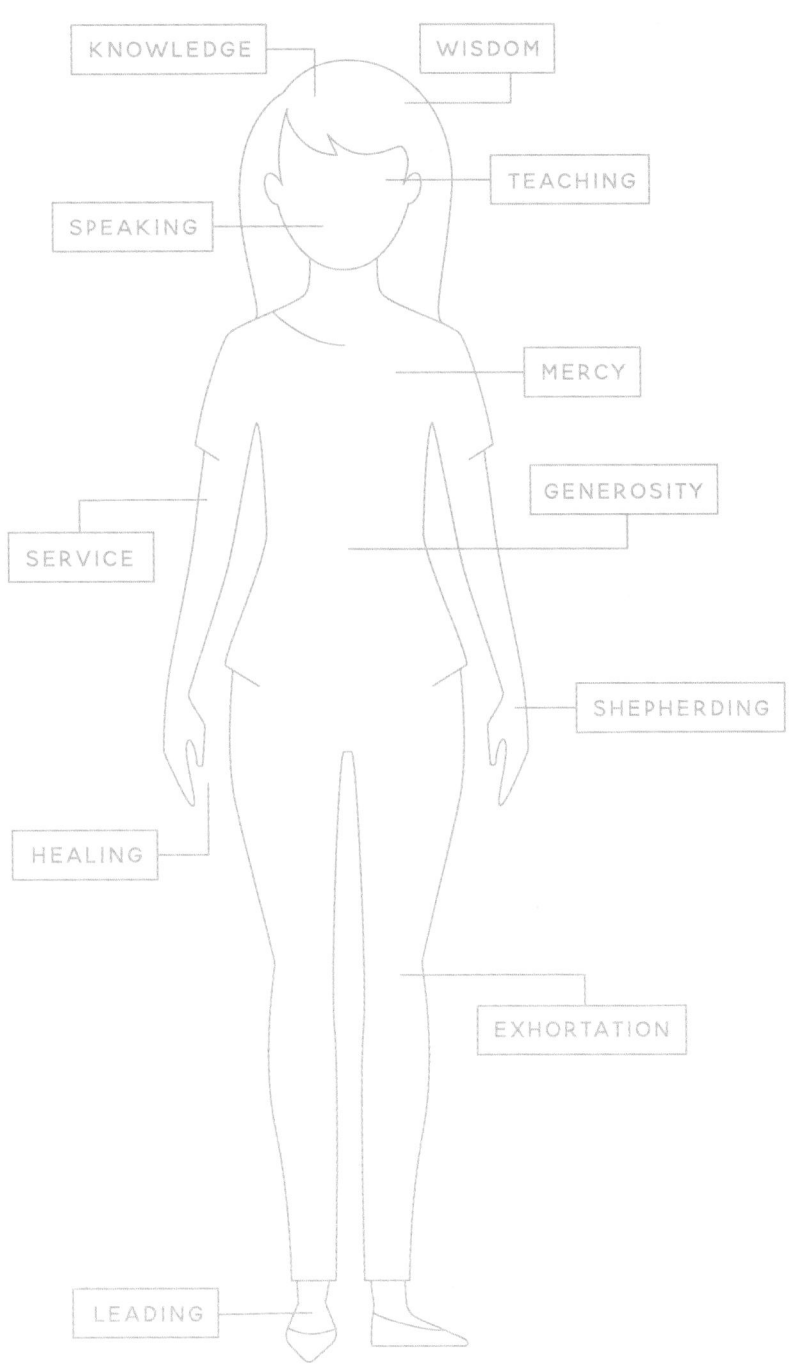

Views of Miraculous Gifts

While some gifts are in line with natural abilities, such as teaching or generosity, others are considered miraculous gifts, such as healing, speaking in tongues, or prophecy. Believers disagree on whether or not spiritual gifts, and especially the miraculous gifts, are active today.

CESSATIONIST

The cessationist view argues that the purpose of the miraculous gifts was to confirm and authenticate the message of the apostles. Through healing, tongues, and miracles, the apostles demonstrated their authority to speak the gospel message. Cessationists believe that because the miraculous gifts were used specifically by the apostles, once the apostles died, the gifts ceased. There are also different degrees in the cessationist view. Some believe that all spiritual gifts have ceased, whereas others believe that only the miraculous gifts of healing, tongues, and miracles have ceased.

CONTINUATIONIST

The continuationist view argues that the miraculous gifts remain active to this day. This view holds that all of the gifts outlined in Scripture are still given by the Holy Spirit and used by believers. Continuationists often point to 1 Corinthians 14, in which Paul speaks specifically about the gifts of tongues and prophecy. They claim that if the gifts ceased with the apostles, Paul would not be giving instructions on carrying out such gifts in the Church. Like the cessationist view, there are also varying degrees in the continuationist view. Some believe that the gift of tongues is a necessary sign of the indwelling of the Holy Spirit, which means all believers possess this gift, while others believe that tongues are a gift of the Spirit given to some, but not all believers. Still, others believe that the Holy Spirit empowers evangelism by signs, tongues, and miracles. Most who hold this view believe that the miraculous gifts must accompany the preaching of the gospel to be accepted by faith. Lastly, there is an open but cautious view in which believers are open to the reality of miraculous gifts but are cautious about making claims over their usage.

APPLICATION

Because Scripture is not clear on the role of miraculous gifts, we should remember that beliefs surrounding the place of miraculous gifts today should not be a cause for division among believers. It is important not to designate one view as "right" and one as "wrong." As believers, we should respect the convictions of our brothers and sisters in Christ, even if we disagree with their views. However, we should also practice discernment with the miraculous gifts. It is important to hold claims about the miraculous gifts against Scripture to determine their truth. Many people have used the miraculous gifts as a way to deceive and take advantage of others, so we must have discerning hearts over those who proclaim to have them.

CESSATIONIST VIEW

The purpose of the miraculous gifts was to confirm and authenticate the message of the apostles; once the apostles died, the gifts ceased.

CONTINUATIONIST VIEW

The miraculous gifts remain active to this day; all of the gifts outlined in Scripture are still given by the Holy Spirit and used by believers.

> IN THIS SECTION

The Universal Church, Regional Church, and Local Church

Visible and Invisible Church

Ordinances and Sacraments

Baptism

Communion

Liturgy

Church Government

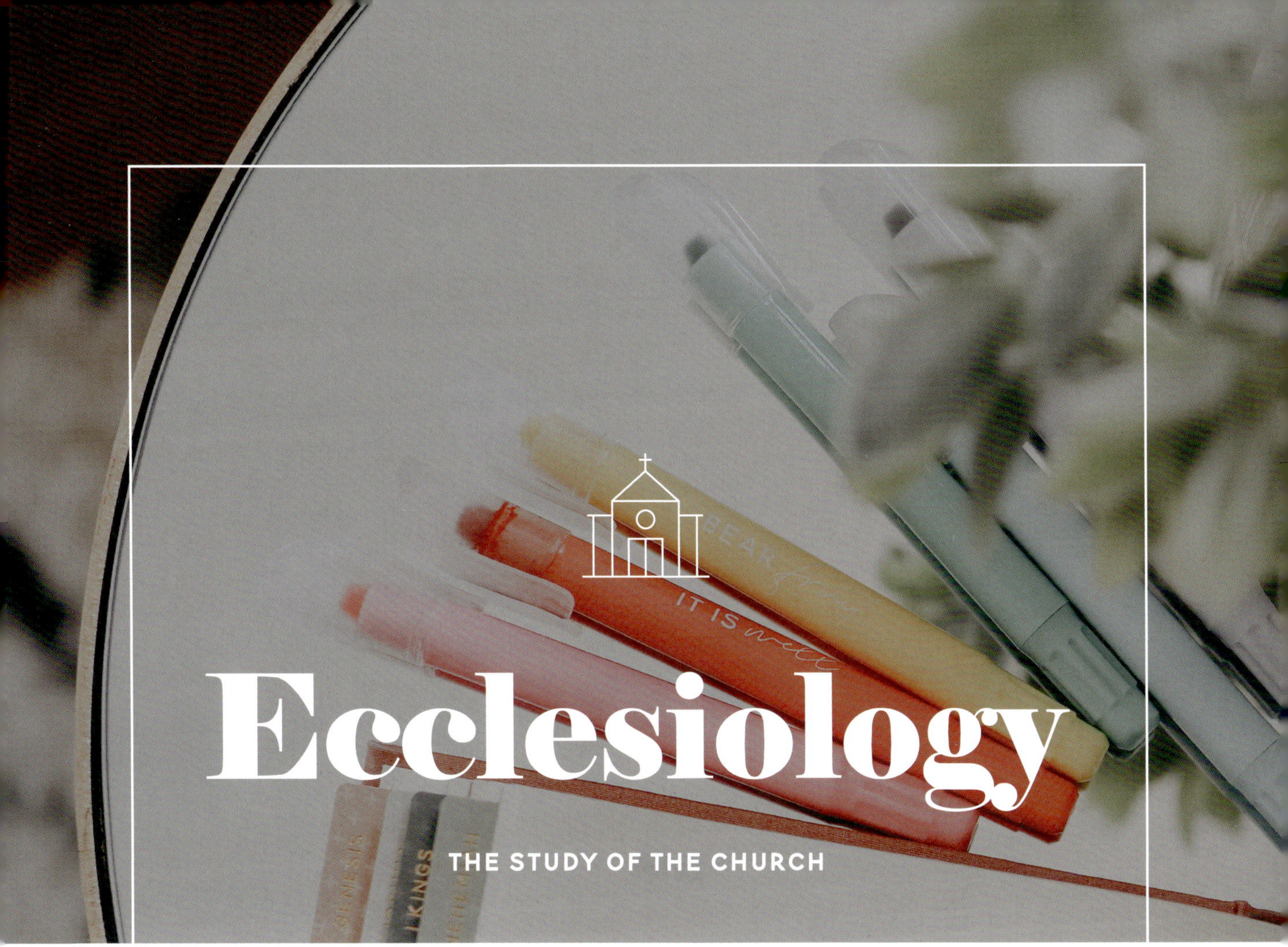

Ecclesiology

THE STUDY OF THE CHURCH

QUESTIONS ANSWERED

What is the Church? | What is the role of baptism and Communion? | How are churches structured?

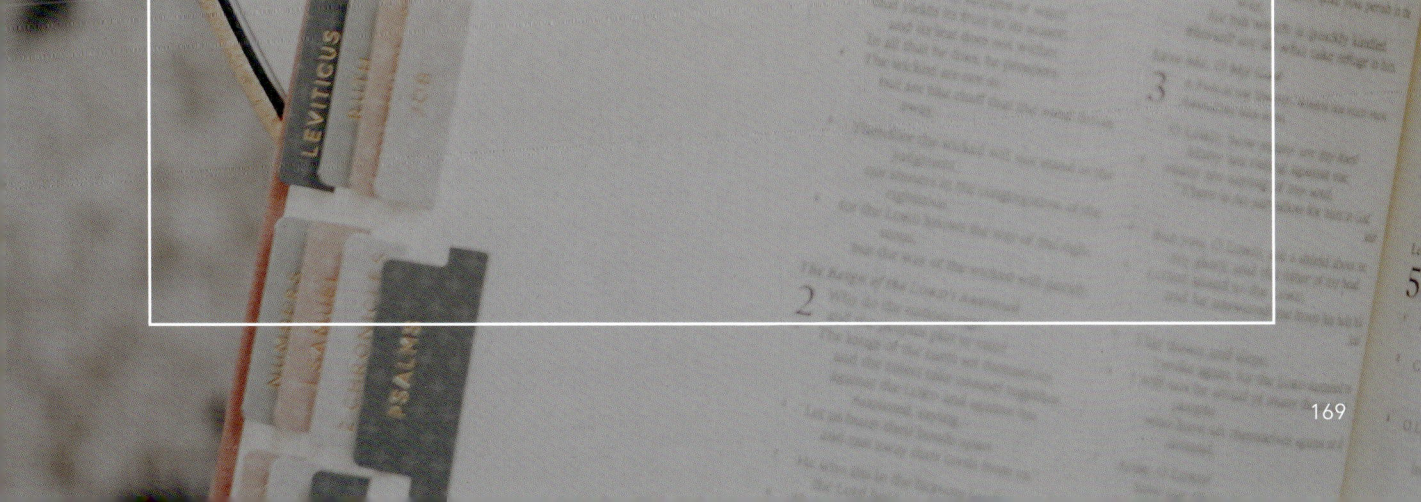

THE UNIVERSAL CHURCH, REGIONAL CHURCH, AND LOCAL CHURCH

The Church is made up of all believers in Jesus Christ. The Church is not a building but the gathering of the people of God. However, when someone talks about "church," they can mean several different things.

UNIVERSAL CHURCH

The Universal Church is composed of every person—throughout history and in every part of the world—who has been saved by grace through faith in Jesus Christ. The word "catholic" is a synonym for "universal." It is sometimes used instead of "universal" to describe the Church (in the Apostles' Creed, for example). However, this is different from when "catholic" is used to describe the Roman Catholic Church. The important thing to remember is that the Universal Church is united under Christ. Despite differences of doctrine over secondary or tertiary issues, every true believer is united under the Church.

LOCAL CHURCH

A local church is a local group of believers who gather regularly under the teaching of God's Word in the name of Jesus Christ, agree upon the primary doctrines of Scripture, and function within a structure of leadership and oversight. The local church is what people most often refer to when they talk about going to church. While local churches often meet in buildings, it is not the building itself that makes up a church but the gathering of believers. It is also important to note that many of the letters in the New Testament were written to local churches.

REGIONAL CHURCH

The regional church is made up of believers in a specific area. An example of the regional church could be "the Mexican Church" or "the Metro-Atlanta Church." Paul addresses a regional church in the book of Galatians when he says, "to the churches in Galatia."

The Church is Christ's bride. Not only does God love His Church, but He also promises to build and protect her (Matthew 16:18). That does not mean that believers within the Church will have easy lives free from persecution. Rather, we know that even death cannot stop God's purposes, and He will protect His Church until He comes again. Christ is the cornerstone or foundation of the Church, and the Bible is its guide. One day, the Church will be gathered together in the presence of Jesus for all of eternity (1 Thessalonians 4:16-17). God will unite us with brothers and sisters in Christ from all around the world—from ages past, present, and future.

APPLICATION

When God saves us, He calls us into fellowship with other believers. Just as we love, serve, and pray for those within our local churches, so those within our church help us in our times of struggle. There is no perfect church, for the Church is made up of sinners just like us, and at times, we will hurt one another. Yet the Church is where we live out the "one-anothers" of our faith—the calls to love one another, forgive one another, and be patient with one another. It is where repentance, church discipline, and church ordinances are practiced. If you are not a member of a local church, use this as motivation to commit to a local, Bible-believing church, and start serving there as soon as possible! Just as God loves His Church, so should we.

THE TRUE CHURCH

VISIBLE AND INVISIBLE CHURCH

When we consider the Church, we must distinguish between the visible church and the invisible church. While these two concepts overlap, they are not the same.

VISIBLE CHURCH

The Visible Church is made up of every person who proclaims faith in Jesus Christ. It is the Church as people on earth see it. However, while many call themselves Christians, there are certainly many who claim the name of Christ but do not have true, saving faith in Him. Someone can be part of the Visible Church but not a true part of the Universal Church.

INVISIBLE CHURCH

The Invisible Church is made up of all those who have true, saving faith in Jesus Christ. It is the Church as God sees it. While the Visible Church includes false teachers, those who seem to fall away, and others who do not possess real faith in Jesus Christ, the Invisible Church is made up only of those who are genuinely saved and will be revealed at Christ's second coming.

Everyone who is a part of the Invisible Church is also part of the Visible Church, but not all who are part of the Visible Church also belong to the Invisible Church. Only God can see the hearts of humans, so although we can have a good idea of those who are truly part of the Invisible Church as we observe fruit in their lives, we cannot know all who belong to the Lord until Christ returns and gathers all believers together.

APPLICATION

Understanding the visible and invisible Church brings us comfort that all who are God's will be gathered together with Him in eternity. It also encourages and urges us to hold fast to the truth of Scripture so that we do not succumb to empty speech or false teaching. This brings importance to the type of teaching we hear and receive as well. We should only accept that which is gospel-centered. We should continually examine our hearts and speak the truth of the gospel to ourselves so that we do not depart from the truth it brings. On a relational level, we should be encouraged to continually share the gospel's truth inside and outside of the Visible Church. Without the complete assurance of who has received genuine and true salvation in Jesus Christ, we must speak truth into one another's lives and take advantage of every opportunity to point to the hope of the gospel.

ORDINANCES AND SACRAMENTS

Ordinances are Christian rites or practices ordained by Jesus Christ in the Bible for believers. They have tangible elements that represent a spiritual reality. There are two ordinances for the Church: baptism and Communion. Some believe these practices are means of grace that spiritually benefit a believer, in which case one would refer to them as sacraments. Others believe these rites are simply symbolic and do not have any unique spiritual benefit, in which case one would refer to the elements as ordinances.

BAPTISM

Baptism is a physical act and visual representation that communicates the inward change of believers who have come to faith in Christ. The water acts as a symbol by signifying the spiritual cleansing from sin for the person being baptized. If done by immersion, the person is placed under the water, visually representing the burial of Christ after His death and the death of that person's former life. Then he or she is brought up out of the water, representing the resurrection of Christ and the new life received. Other methods of baptism exist, including baptism that takes place through the sprinkling of water. Regardless of the method used, it is important to understand that baptism does not bring salvation to the person being baptized; instead, it is a mark of their salvation. We should be careful not to view baptism as the means for our salvation but as a beautiful display of the faith of the one being baptized.

APPLICATION

Baptism is not only a response to one's salvation in Christ, but it also brings about accountability in the life of the believer. It is a public act because it is done in the eyes of the people who will hold the person being baptized accountable for living out their faith. It is not just a public display of faith; it is also an invitation for the church community to join this person in helping them walk in faith. As we continue to grow in our faith, we can look back at our baptism, not as the means of our salvation but as evidence of our salvation that encourages us to continue walking in the newness of life we have found in Christ.

ECCLESIOLOGY *Ordinances and Sacraments: Baptism*

BAPTISM
A Display of Faith

1. WATER
Signifies the spiritual cleansing from sin

3. BROUGHT UP
Represents the resurrection of Christ and the new life received

2. BY IMMERSION
A visual representation of Christ's burial and the death of the believer's former life

TWO VIEWS ON BAPTISM

PAEDOBAPTISM	CREDOBAPTISM
Allows for baptism of those who have not made a profession of faith (typically infants).	Allows for baptism of only those who have made a profession of faith.
Believes that the new covenant brought about by Christ includes believers and nonbelievers.	Believes that the new covenant includes only professing believers in Christ.
Baptism is a sign of the entrance into the new covenant.	Baptist is a public testimony of the profession of faith — a sign of a regenerated heart.

COMMUNION & THE PASSOVER

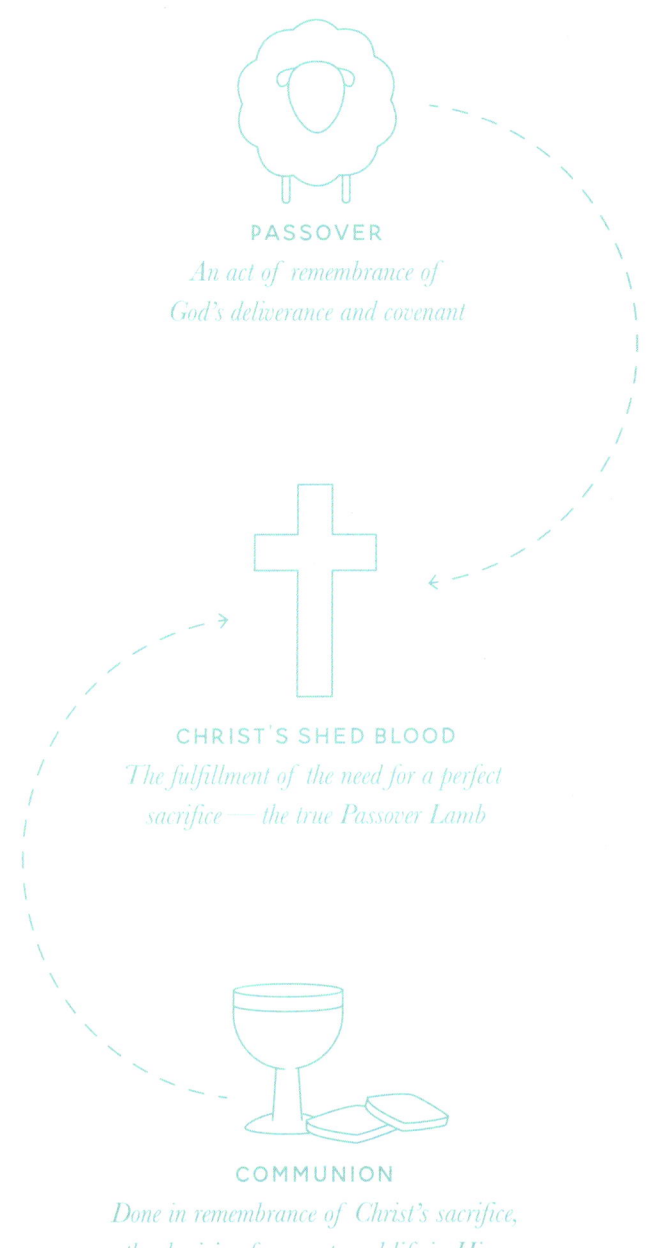

PASSOVER
An act of remembrance of God's deliverance and covenant

CHRIST'S SHED BLOOD
The fulfillment of the need for a perfect sacrifice — the true Passover Lamb

COMMUNION
Done in remembrance of Christ's sacrifice, thanksgiving for our eternal life in Him, and hopeful expectation for His coming again

COMMUNION

Communion is an outward display of the gospel that believers practice regularly in remembrance of what Christ did for us on the cross. Also known as the Lord's Supper, Communion was first initiated by Christ as He ate the Passover meal with His disciples on the night He was betrayed and handed over to die (Matthew 26:26-30). As Christ demonstrated for His disciples at this meal, when we take the bread and wine of Communion, we remember the broken body and shed blood of our Lord, which allows us to stand righteous before Him and be restored to fellowship with Him. Participating in Communion identifies us as belonging to the redeemed people of God. It calls us to look back to the death of our Savior. It calls us to look presently to Jesus as our nourishment through whom we have eternal life (John 6:53-58). And finally, it calls us to look forward to the marriage banquet between Christ and His Church—to the feast that is to come when He returns to call us home as His bride (Matthew 26:29, Luke 22:30, Revelation 19:9).

APPLICATION

As we take Communion in our churches with other believers, we do so to remember the suffering and death of our Savior, yet there is much more we remember as we partake of the elements. Practicing Communion does not save us but should only be practiced by those who have professed Jesus as their Lord and Savior. We come to the table of Communion, broken over our sin—but understanding that though it was our sin that sent Jesus to the cross, it was Christ's victory on the cross that brings us to the table. As we break the bread and drink from the cup, we dwell on the faithfulness of our Savior. Though we were once enemies of God, even in our sin, He has reconciled us to Himself and made us a part of His family. On the day that Christ returns, believers will sit with Christ at the most magnificent banquet table of all. All people of every tribe, tongue, and nation who have loved God will gather at this table and feast with the final Passover Lamb—the One whose death paid for our sins. What incredible joy that day will hold for us when all things will be made right, and the curse of sin and death will be no more.

Differing Views of Communion

Communion is a visible sign or seal of the promises of the gospel to us. However, there is a variety of views regarding the degree to which Christ's presence is involved as believers partake of Communion. Here are some basic descriptions of each view.

TRANSUBSTANTIATION

Transubstantiation is the traditional Catholic view regarding the essence of the elements in Communion. The Catholic Church believes that as the priest elevates the bread and wine and recites the story of the Lord's Supper, the substance of the elements physically changes to the literal blood and body of Jesus. The change is not perceptible to a person as they take the elements and consume them; nonetheless, it has occurred. Protestant Christians reject this view on the grounds that it suggests that Christ's physical body and blood need to be sacrificed repeatedly for the forgiveness of sins, an idea that contradicts Scripture's claims that Christ's sacrificial work on the cross for sin is final and complete (Hebrews 9:24-26).

CONSUBSTANTIATION

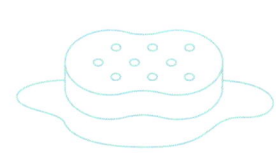

Consubstantiation is derived from Martin Luther's beliefs of Communion, and the Lutheran denomination holds this view. Many people see consubstantiation as lying halfway between the Roman Catholic and Reformed views of the Lord's Supper. Instead of believing that the elements actually become the physical body of Jesus, Lutherans believe that Jesus Christ is uniquely present in, with, and under the bread and the wine whenever the Lord's Supper is celebrated. There is no mystical change to the bread and wine, but when the church celebrates Communion, His physical body and blood are present with the elements. This view is often compared to a sponge soaked in water. The sponge is not the water, and the water is not the sponge, but the two are there together.

ECCLESIOLOGY *Differing Views of Communion*

SYMBOLIC OR MEMORIAL VIEW

Ulrich Zwingli, an early Swiss Reformer, is credited with the view of Communion that many Baptists commonly hold in the Protestant Church. Zwingli emphasized that the Lord's Supper is only a sign or memorial for the believer to celebrate in remembrance of Christ. The broken bread and wine help the church remember that His body was broken and His blood was shed. Still, when Jesus established Communion, He used bread and wine to represent His body figuratively, not literally. Protestants who hold this view believe that while Jesus has promised to be with us always, He is not physically present as Communion is practiced.

SPIRITUAL PRESENCE VIEW

The Spiritual Presence view is attributed to John Calvin. He rejected both the Catholic belief that the elements change into the physical body and blood of Jesus and Zwingli's belief that Communion is only a memorial. Calvin believed that when the Church celebrates the Lord's Supper, Jesus is spiritually present in a special way. While He is not physically there, His church communes with Him as they partake of the elements.

LITURGY

The word "liturgy" means "the service." Whether or not a church uses this terminology, every church abides by a certain order that they follow in their worship service from week to week. A fuller definition for liturgy could be "the order of service." In some denominations, this order of service is much more structured. For example, in Presbyterian churches, the order of service is usually passed out in a bulletin so each church member can follow along. It might include a welcome from the pastor, announcements for the congregation, a call to worship, selected hymns, and prayers of confession and praise for the service. On the other hand, a non-denominational church, for example, may have a less official order that the congregation expects week by week. Instead, each week may include a welcome, greeting, songs of worship, sermon, and ending prayer. Many components create a liturgy, and one church's liturgy can look very different from another.

APPLICATION

As you participate in your congregational gathering from week to week, know that each part of the service has a purpose. Your pastor and church leaders have taken time to develop it for your spiritual growth and edification. Instead of going through the motions as you sit in your church on another Sunday morning, take time to notice each element of the service. Thank the Lord for each part of the service, and think about how each part glorifies Him and helps you love Him more. Thank Him for the people who contribute to your church's gathering. As you begin to notice the time and intentionality behind your church's liturgy, you will care more about all the elements you participate in from week to week.

> THANK THE LORD FOR EACH PART OF THE SERVICE, AND THINK ABOUT HOW EACH PART GLORIFIES HIM AND HELPS YOU LOVE HIM MORE.

CHURCH GOVERNMENT

Just as countries or cities have governmental structures, churches function under church governments. From the beginning of the early church, leaders have been in place to shepherd believers. The New Testament provides two main categories of leaders for churches to follow. One is the position of "elder" or "overseer" or "pastor." Each of these terms is used to describe the same role. Another position given was the "deacon," a role that specifically oversees mercy ministry to serve those in need. While most Protestant denominations have elder and deacon positions, there are various structures for how believers choose to carry out church government. No matter the particular structure to which your church adheres, the purpose should be the same. Church leadership exists to guide, protect, teach, equip, and serve the body of Christ. These positions of leadership are not random or man-made. God ordained them for the edification of His people. No church leadership is perfect, but by the grace and power of the gospel, church government can serve as a beautiful display of the lovingkindness and tender care of our Heavenly Father toward us.

APPLICATION

As followers of Jesus, we are called to honor, love, and even submit to one another (Ephesians 5:21). The believer's life is one of daily submission to God. We follow the example of Christ, the King of kings, who humbled Himself from His heavenly position and became a servant to the very people He created (Philippians 2). Church government is another area of authority to which the believer is commanded to submit. When we submit to those whom the Lord has placed in authority over us, we can healthfully contribute and engage in our congregations. It is important to note here that there will be times when church governments fail and make decisions contrary to the Word of God. Our first place of submission is to the Lord. If human authorities ask us to disobey God, we are not to do so. However, if we are concerned with decisions being made by our church government, we should approach them with humility and loving concern, not out of pride or selfish ambition. In most scenarios, those in church government earnestly seek to honor the Lord and their congregation in every decision they make. There is an enormous amount of time and effort that goes into governing a body of believers. We must pray for our church's leaders, encourage them, and thank them for their work to lead us more toward Christ.

ECCLESIOLOGY *Church Government*

EPISCOPAL GOVERNMENT

This type of government gives the power of decision-making to the leading bishop or pastor of the church. This style of leadership is practiced by Eastern Orthodox, Roman Catholic, Anglican, and Lutheran churches.

CONGREGATIONAL GOVERNMENT

While churches that practice a style of congregational government often have elders and deacons in positions of authority, the power of decision-making is still found in the congregation. In this type of government, the members of the church vote on major decisions. This style of leadership is practiced in many Baptist churches today.

PRESBYTERIAN GOVERNMENT

Presbyterian government places the power of decision-making in the hands of a team of elders elected by the congregation. The elected body of elders is called a session. Sessions from multiple churches make up Presbyteries, and those presbyteries make up the general assembly for an entire denomination.

ELDER

Elders are overseers of the church who shepherd and teach God's people (Acts 20:28). The qualifications for elders can be found in 1 Timothy 3:1-7 and Titus 1:7-9.

DEACON

Deacons support the elders of the church by serving the church body in a variety of ways. Qualifications for deacons are very similar to those of elders, but they do not teach (1 Timothy 3:8-12).

MODELS OF CHURCH GOVERNMENT

Episcopal Government

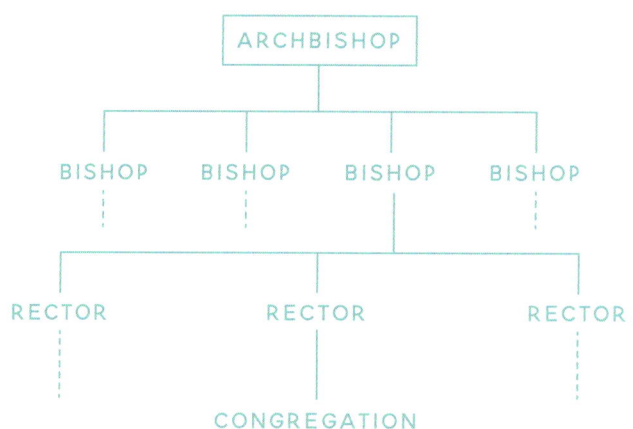

ECCLESIOLOGY *Church Government*

Presbyterian Government

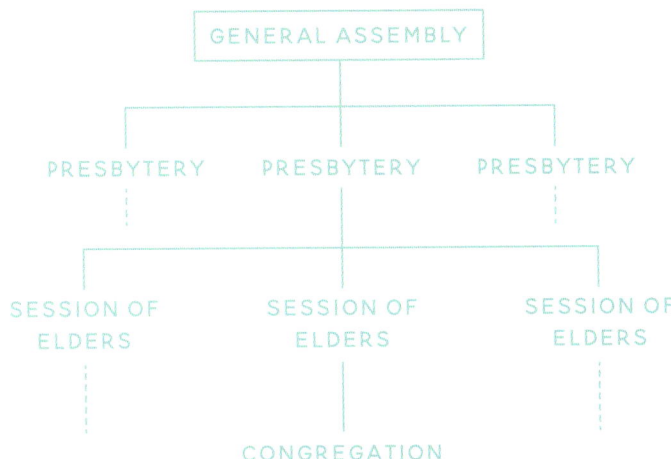

Congregational Government

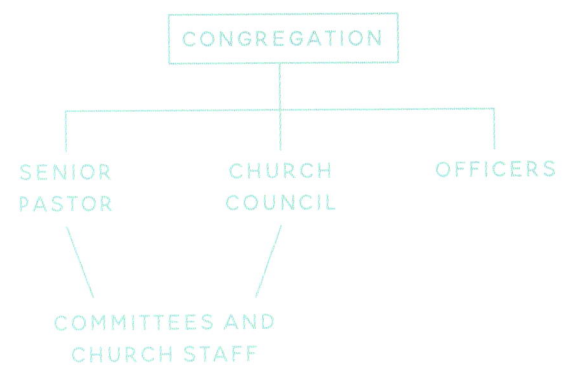

> IN THIS SECTION

Angels

Demons

Angelology

THE STUDY OF ANGELS AND DEMONS

QUESTIONS ANSWERED

What are angels? | *What are demons?* | *Is there a spiritual realm we cannot see?*

ANGELS

The word "angel" appears throughout the Bible more than 200 times and means "messenger." Other references to angelic and heavenly beings under different titles include "cherubim," "seraphim," and "holy ones" (Genesis 3:24, Isaiah 6:2, Psalm 89:5). Angels are spiritual beings who are righteous, powerful, and full of wisdom (2 Samuel 14:20, Psalm 103:20, Revelation 14:10). While Scripture does not address how God created them or what their exact nature is like, it does tell us a good deal about what they do. Angels stand in the presence of God and worship Him. They also guard the presence of God from those not fit to come before Him. Angels work in the world around us by bringing God's Word and delivering His messages, fighting the battles of God, executing His judgments, and protecting and ministering to God's people. While angels are presently superior to us in this world, they will not be in the next. When we are united with God in eternity, that world will primarily belong to followers of Christ, not angels. Angels who did not rebel against God with Satan do not need the salvation provided by Jesus because they are righteous. When Satan and other angels fell from heaven, not every angel was doomed to judgment. They are unlike human beings who are born fallen because of Adam and Eve's sin. Scripture says that angels are spectators of God's unfolding plan of redemption for His people, and they look down at the Church in wonder, learning of our salvation (1 Peter 1:10-12).

APPLICATION

Because we live in a world that is skeptical about things unseen, many people, even Christians, do not think much about angels or the spiritual world at all. And yet, angels are referenced many times throughout the Bible, and we are told that they are actively working among God's people. We should not worship angels or let thoughts of them consume us, but it is helpful and sobering to consider them and their work and what it means for believers. The existence of angels reminds us that there is much more going on in the world around us than we realize. Their temporary superiority over us also points us to the riches we have in salvation through Christ. Christ lowered Himself for a time below the angels to become human and die for the sins of His people. When He rose again and ascended to the Father, He resumed His place above the angels. One day, Christ will bring us into our heavenly home, and we will be in a position above the angels because He has placed His righteousness upon us.

ACTIONS OF ANGELS

DELIVER GOD'S WORD
Luke 1:26-28

FIGHT GOD'S BATTLES
1 Samuel 4:4
Matthew 26:53

GUARD THE PRESENCE OF GOD
Genesis 3:24

ἄγγελος

ANGEL | *angelos* | Messenger

PROTECT AND MINISTER TO GOD'S PEOPLE
Psalm 91:11
Hebrews 1:14

STAND IN GOD'S PRESENCE AND WORSHIP HIM
Revelation 7:11

EXECUTE GOD'S JUDGMENTS
Genesis 19
Exodus 12:23

ACTIONS OF DEMONS

WHAT DEMONS CAN DO:	WHAT DEMONS CANNOT DO:
POSSESS	SEPARATE US FROM THE LOVE OF GOD
OPRESS	THWART GOD'S PLANS
INFLUENCE MEN	REMOVE BELIEVERS FROM GOD'S HAND

DEMONS

While all angels God created were originally good, some rebelled against God and fell from righteousness. Unlike mankind, there is no hope or salvation for them. They have been doomed since their fall and are known as demons (Matthew 25:41). This fall likely happened before Adam and Eve rebelled against God as the serpent who tempted them was Satan, the leader of all demons (Genesis 3:1, Revelation 12:9, Matthew 12:24). Demons support Satan in his work against the kingdom of God. Satan is known as "the ruler of this world" for this very reason (John 14:30). Everything of the world opposes everything of God, and Satan and his demons influence people and nations against God. We read in Scripture that they can also possess people and animals, and we have no reason to believe this does not continue today (Luke 22:3, Mark 5). Satan and his demons are strong and powerful, but they are no match for Jesus. One day, Satan and all of the angels who followed him into rebellion will be cast into the lake of fire.

APPLICATION

As we journey in this world and spread the gospel, we will face attacks from Satan and his demons. If we belong to Christ, we have become Satan's enemies. It is not wise to look at every difficulty we face and see it as demonic oppression, but we also must not forget that demonic oppression exists and certainly works against the kingdom of God. And while Satan and his demons could crush us in an instant, they can now do no such thing because we belong to the King of kings. He has authority over these demonic, evil beings, and they fear Him and want to flee from Him (Matthew 8:29-30). Jesus has defeated Satan and his demons by dying on the cross and rising again, and He has enabled us by His strength to escape Satan's temptations (Colossians 2:15, James 4:7, 1 John 4:4). However, the world around us is influenced by Satan since he is "the prince of this world." When we see deep darkness and disorder, it reminds us that there is an unseen spiritual battle all around us. Though it may be tempting to view people as enemies who display and act out evil, we must remember that the real enemy is the one working behind the scenes, oppressing these people from the truth. The wonderful news is that Satan does not win, no matter how perseverant he is against God and His people. Jesus is victorious.

IN THIS SECTION

Final Judgment

New Heaven and New Earth

Resurrection from the Dead

Heaven

Hell

Four Millennial Views

Eschatology

THE STUDY OF THE END TIMES

QUESTIONS ANSWERED

What will happen when the world ends? | *When is Jesus coming back?* | *Are we in the end times?*

ARE YOU WASHED IN THE BLOOD?
Elisha A. Hoffman, 1878

Have you been to Jesus for the cleansing power?
Are you washed in the blood of the Lamb?
Are you fully trusting in His grace this hour?
Are you washed in the blood of the Lamb?

REFRAIN
Are you washed in the blood,
In the soul-cleansing blood of the Lamb?
Are your garments spotless? Are they white as snow?
Are you washed in the blood of the Lamb?

Are you walking daily by the Savior's side?
Are you washed in the blood of the Lamb?
Do you rest each moment in the Crucified?
Are you washed in the blood of the Lamb?

When the Bridegroom cometh will your robes be white?
Are you washed in the blood of the Lamb?
Will your soul be ready for the mansions bright,
And be washed in the blood of the Lamb?

Lay aside the garments that are stained with sin,
And be washed in the blood of the Lamb;
There's a fountain flowing for the soul unclean,
Oh, be washed in the blood of the Lamb!

FINAL JUDGMENT

The Final Judgment refers to the judgment that will occur when Jesus returns to judge the living and the dead. Each person appropriately receives eternity in heaven with Christ or eternal separation from Him. Although the timing of Christ's return is yet unknown (Matthew 24:36), some of the events that will take place then, during "the judgment on the great day" (Jude 6), are provided in Scripture. John 5:28-29 tells us that the dead will be raised, and the Lord will rightly judge all: "a time is coming when all who are in the graves will hear his voice and come out—those who have done good things, to the resurrection of life, but those who have done wicked things, to the resurrection of condemnation." It is God's perfect holiness and righteousness that justly demands this perfect justice. When the curtain falls on human history and God comes to judge the world, He will fulfill His plan for final redemption.

On this day, we will stand trial before Christ, in a court higher and grander than any other. All the world will go before our true judge as He presents His case with what is written in the books and the Lamb's Book of Life (Revelation 20:12). And when the evidence is presented, it will remain beyond dispute—there will be no argument, sympathy, or defense. No one can appeal the sentence—no one can step in to defend. For all that will be is God's perfect and final judgment.

APPLICATION

While this will be a somber "day of wrath" (Romans 2:5) for lost sinners, what hope and joy exist for believers who have nothing to fear on that day. Through Jesus's death and resurrection, God finalized for us what we could never have done for ourselves. He took the weight of our sins and offered Himself as a perfect sacrifice for us, taking our place so that when the final judgment comes, those who are saved can rejoice in the truth that the blood of the Lamb covers their sins. God will not see our sin on that final judgment day—sin that would otherwise condemn us to hell. Instead, God will see His Son in us, who is blameless in every way.

Standing in such knowledge of God's grace, we should come to God in humble adoration for what He has done—that it is only in His kindness (Titus 3:4-5) that we escape torment in separation from Christ for all eternity. We can boast not at all in ourselves but in Christ, who is our Savior. Furthermore, rather than keeping this truth to ourselves, we bear witness of this truth to those around us—those we live with, those we work with, those we hold dear or meet in passing. We share with them our treasure—the way to true life—so that they too may receive a crown of glory when Christ separates those who love Him from those He never knew (Matthew 7:21-23).

NEW HEAVEN AND NEW EARTH

One day, Jesus is returning to earth. Though the earth as we know it will be no more, Jesus will restore and renew creation. The new heaven and new earth refer to the redemption of creation upon Jesus's return and final judgment. The use of the word "new" comes as a result of Christ's work to redeem and restore creation at His second coming. Jesus Christ came to make all things new. He came to reveal the will of God so that creation would be restored to its original design and purpose. He came to reverse the curse of sin and fulfill God's promise to His people to send them a Savior. All of these things needed to be accomplished so that God's people could dwell in the presence of God for eternity. The new heavens and new earth are painted as a vision in Revelation 21:1-2, "Then I saw a new heaven and a new earth; for the first heaven and the first earth had passed away, and the sea was no more. I also saw the holy city, the new Jerusalem, coming down out of heaven from God, prepared like a bride adorned for her husband." Though we could never possibly imagine what the new heaven and new earth will look like, we know that all believers will one day set eyes upon it on the day that Christ returns.

APPLICATION

The Bible begins and ends with the state of creation. Genesis introduces God's intentions for creation, and Revelation speaks to its renewal. The beauty of the gospel story is that Jesus Christ came to restore all that was broken and make it new. This offers us hope. Everything on this earth is temporal and will not last. 2 Corinthians 5:1-2 reminds us, "For we know that if our earthly tent we live in is destroyed, we have a building from God, an eternal dwelling in the heavens, not made with hands. Indeed, we groan in this tent, desiring to put on our heavenly dwelling." All of the sin-ridden effects of our rebellion will not be the final say for those who put their faith in Jesus Christ. They will be offered a new life in Him, and with that new life comes a new dwelling place when Jesus returns—a perfect dwelling place in the new heavens and new earth when God will be with His people forever. Not only does this encourage us through devastation, hardship, and trials of every kind, but it encourages us to bring as many people with us as possible by sharing the redemptive hope of the gospel. When Christ says that He will make creation new, that includes us (2 Corinthians 5:17).

ESCHATOLOGY *New Heaven and New Earth*

EDEN TO ETERNITY

When God created the world, it was good, but it was not yet all that it could be. In the garden of Eden, God gave Adam and Eve commands to fill the earth with image-bearers and work and subdue the earth. As God's representatives, they would continue God's work, and the world would change for it. When sin entered the world, the world was corrupted, and that good work was frustrated. The world is no longer as it should be, but God has not given up on His original intention for creation. When Jesus comes, He will bring a new creation, and all that Eden was meant to grow and develop into will come to pass at last.

THE GARDEN OF EDEN	THE NEW CREATION
Adam and Eve walked with God *(Genesis 3:8)*	God dwells with us *(Revelation 21:3)*
The Garden-Temple	The Lord is the temple *(Revelation 21:22)*
Adam and Eve given the command to fill the earth with image-bearers *(Genesis 1:28a)*	Image-bearers from every tribe, tongue, and nation gathered *(Revelation 7:9)*
Adam and Eve were naked *(Genesis 2:25)*	Clothed in righteousness *(Revelation 19:8)*
The sun and moon separate night and day *(Genesis 1:14)*	The glory of God is the light *(Revelation 21:23)*
Marriage of Adam and Eve *(Genesis 2:24)*	Marriage of Christ and the Church *(Revelation 21:2)*
The First Adam vulnerable to the the serpent (the devil) *(Genesis 3)*	The Second Adam, Jesus, crushed the head of the serpent *(Genesis 3:15)*
The tree of life is off-limits *(Genesis 2:17)*	The tree of life brings healing *(Revelation 22:2)*
The curse of sin corrupted Eden *(Genesis 3)*	The curse is replaced with blessing *(Revelation 22:3)*

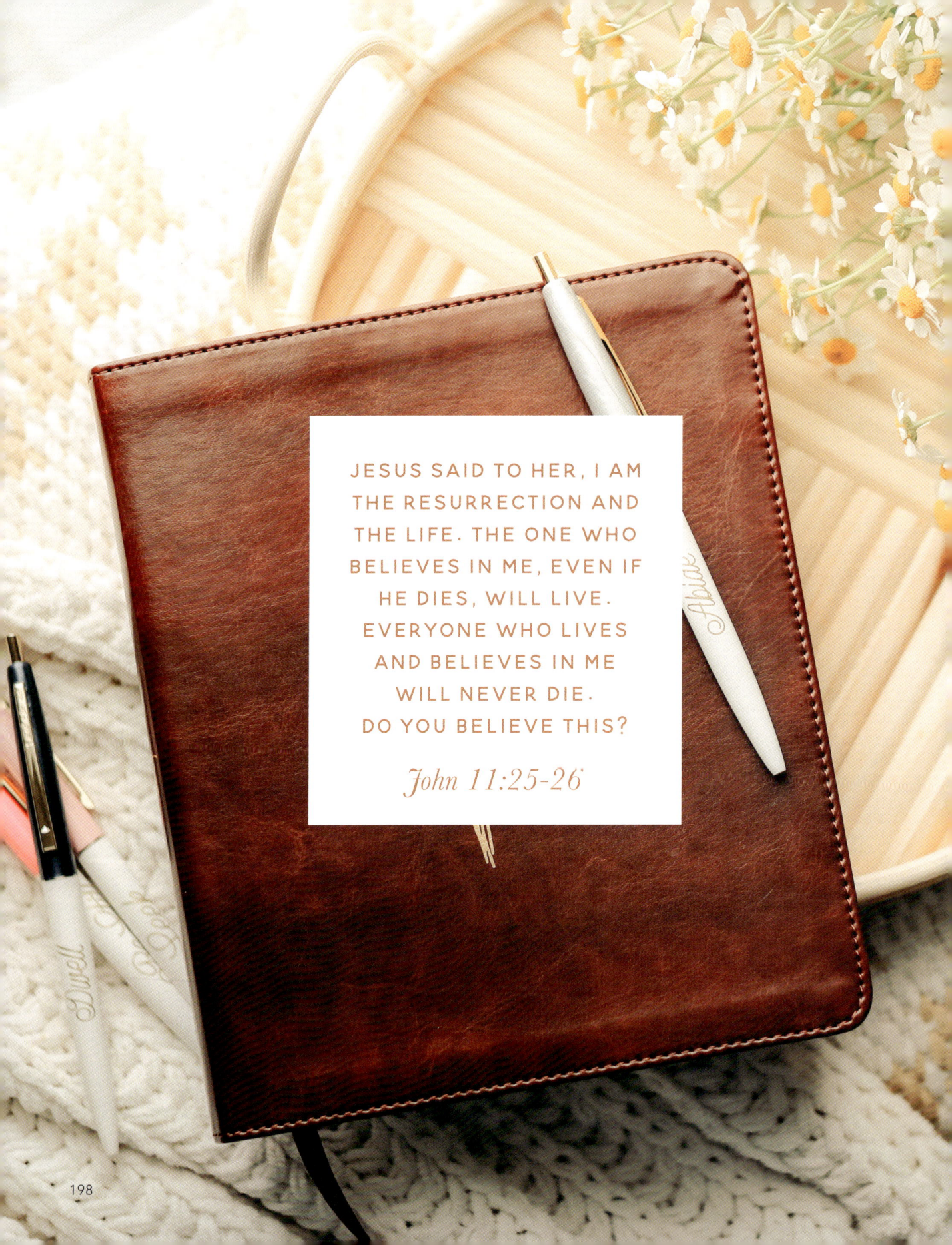

RESURRECTION FROM THE DEAD

In the Old Testament, Job asked, "When a person dies, will he come back to life? If so, I would wait all the days of my struggle until my relief comes" (Job 14:14). Though Job originally asked his question thousands of years ago, it is still a common concern today. What happens after we die? Is this life all that there is? Thankfully, through the Bible, we know the answer to these questions. Unless the Lord returns soon, we will all die a physical death. In the same way, we will all rise from the dead with resurrected bodies and souls when Christ returns. During His life and ministry, Jesus demonstrated that He has the power to raise the dead from the grave (John 11:25). To the astonishment of His followers, Jesus publicly raised His friend Lazarus from the dead, as well as a little girl who had passed away (John 11:38-44, Mark 5:35-43). And Jesus Himself rose from the dead after dying on the cross. Indeed, it is because Jesus rose again that we have hope for the resurrection of our mortal bodies. For those who trust in Jesus, our resurrection will be a new life with God. For those who do not, it will be complete separation from God for all of eternity.

APPLICATION

This world is not our home. Though we will suffer in this life, and our bodies will break down, we can have confidence that this is not the end of our story. One day, we will live in perfect bodies, free from pain and suffering. We wait eagerly for this day, as it says in Romans 8:23: "Not only that, but we ourselves who have the Spirit as the firstfruits—we also groan within ourselves, eagerly waiting for adoption, the redemption of our bodies." While we should take care of our bodies today to serve the Lord and others, we should not be consumed by our appearances, for these earthly bodies will waste away. The beauty encouraged in Scripture is that of inward adornment, wholeheartedly pursuing the Lord. This pursuit will never be in vain. Although these physical bodies fade, we have hope that we will one day see Christ face to face as we stand before Him in our new, glorified bodies.

HEAVEN

When we hear the word "heaven," we likely have images in our mind of disembodied spirits in the clouds with the angels. When the Bible talks about heaven, it primarily refers to the new heaven and new earth, a physical new creation that Christ will establish when He returns. However, the Bible does mention another state of being that exists in the time between death and resurrection, which theologians call the intermediate state. Our knowledge of this state is limited, but we do know that until Jesus's second coming, we will still be awaiting bodily resurrection after we die. It is only when He returns that He will raise us with new, heavenly bodies. However, Scripture like 2 Corinthians 5:8 and Luke 23:43 imply that we will somehow be present with God until then, though not bodily. Indeed our bodies will perish, yet our souls will find complete peace, joy, and rest in God.

APPLICATION

As Christians, we can face death with a sure hope without fear. Because of our faith in the saving work of Jesus Christ, we know that our intermediate state will be one of complete satisfaction in the Lord's presence. Our souls will witness the full wonder and majesty of Jesus in heaven. We will not be bound to death, awaiting final judgment and God's wrath for our sin (Revelation 20:11-15). Rather, we will be awaiting our bodily resurrection, the restoration, and glorification of our physical selves when Jesus returns to earth as King (1 Corinthians 15:51-53). Then, the intermediate state will come to a sweet conclusion when we enter the new heavens and the new earth, coming into the fullness of God's kingdom (Revelation 21:1-3).

ELEMENTS OF HEAVEN

ETERNAL PRESENCE OF GOD

JUDGED ACCORDING TO CHRIST'S RIGHTEOUSNESS

PEACE

ESCHATOLOGY *Heaven, Hell*

HELL

While heaven is eternity with God, hell is eternal separation from Him. Heaven is full of blessing, whereas hell is void of inheritance, joy, and rest. The horror of hell is figuratively described as a lake of fire (Revelation 20:15) and a place of darkness with weeping and gnashing of teeth (Matthew 8:12). Those who reject the gospel of Jesus will face a judgment that results in eternity in hell. The punishment that unbelievers will face in hell is also eternal, never to be lifted. There will be no opportunity for repentance after the final judgment. The punishment of hell speaks to the seriousness of sin and the rejection of a Holy God. Sin deserves penalty, and without the forgiveness of sin, there can be no hope for eternity with Christ.

APPLICATION

The reality of hell brings weightiness to our evangelism. Many of us are nervous to tell others about hell—it is often easier to pass over the subject. But as believers, we must be bold to share all aspects of the gospel, including the consequence of not believing it. While Christians are called to spread the good news of the gospel, if we only speak about His love and not the seriousness of our sin, then we downplay the gravity of hell. We must not be like other people who disregard the existence of hell. By the grace of God, we have been rescued from this fate, and we should adamantly share the gospel with others so that they can be rescued as well. The horrors of hell should deeply burden our hearts for the lost and propel us to speak the gospel in every opportunity that we are given.

ELEMENTS OF HELL

ETERNAL SEPARATION FROM GOD

JUDGED ACCORDING TO MAN'S SINFULNESS

GRIEF

FOUR MILLENNIAL VIEWS

Many questions likely arise when considering details regarding the end of the world. While we cannot be entirely sure of all that will take place, this God-given curiosity drives us to the Creator of time—the One who has much to say about the end times in His Word. The Lord has graciously revealed to us what is coming at the end of His redemptive story in Scripture. While there are many unknown details, we can be sure that God is victorious, and His people from all generations will be reunited with Him. The most important event that will take place at the end of the world is the return of Christ. In Revelation 20, the Apostle John describes 1,000 years during which Jesus will reign over the earth. Many Christians refer to this time as "the millennium" or "the millennial kingdom." While the ultimate purpose of this passage in Revelation is to point us to the hope and security we have in Christ, there are many different beliefs regarding when and how this millennium will occur in relation to Jesus's second coming. Four major views held within the Church include amillennialism, postmillennialism, classical premillennialism, and dispensational premillennialism.

AMILLENNIALISM

Amillennialists believe that the millennium referenced in Revelation 21 is a figurative period of time—not a literal thousand-year kingdom. Amillennialists believe that this thousand-year period refers to the present age and that we currently live in the millennium. Christ is King, and He is reigning, but He is reigning from heaven. This period was inaugurated from heaven at His ascension, and it will be consummated at His second coming. Amillennialists see the victory and suffering that believers face in this age as aligning with Revelation's description of the millennium. They also believe that Satan is currently bound and cannot prevent the spread of the gospel in the world, but he can try to harm the Church. Amillennialists would also say that our current age can be captured by the phrase "the already and not yet." Jesus presently reigns, but His kingdom will be fully realized when He comes at the end of this era and reigns eternally in the new heavens and new earth.

POSTMILLENNIALISM

Postmillennialists agree with amillennialists in their belief that the millennium is a period of time that is figurative and not literal. They also agree on the basic sequence of events during the last days of the world: Christ's return, the general resurrection of both the righteous and the wicked, the final judgment, and the beginning of the new heavens and new earth. They also both agree that Satan is currently bound but will be briefly released toward the end of the millennium to cause rebellion against Christ. However, while amillennialists believe that Christians will experience both suffering and victory before the return of Christ, postmillennialists believe that Christians will increasingly gain influence and experience mostly victory toward the end of the world. The world will become more and more open to the gospel, and there will be a period of great righteousness and peace before Jesus returns to the earth.

CLASSICAL PREMILLENNIALISM

Christians who hold the classical premillennialism view believe that Jesus will come back after a tribulation period in the world. He will raise all believers to be with Him, and then He will reign over the earth in a millennial kingdom with them for 1,000 years. They believe the millennial kingdom is not a figurative period of time; it is a literal amount of time that is yet to occur. During Christ's millennial reign, Satan will be bound in a pit, but he will briefly be released at the end of the millennium, causing some people to rebel against Christ. The Lord will end this rebellion, and there will be a resurrection for all of the wicked who will then face the final judgment. After this judgment, the new heavens and new earth will begin.

DISPENSATIONAL PREMILLENNIALISM

The key difference between classical premillennialism and dispensational premillennialism is that Jesus will rapture believers before a period of tribulation. This tribulation period is known as the "great tribulation," which will be seven years of satanic influence on the earth that will progressively get worse and worse. Jesus will rapture all who believe in Him before this period of time, and then He will return with His saints after this period ends. Then Christ will set up His millennial kingdom. The events that follow this follow the same sequence as those described in classical premillennialism.

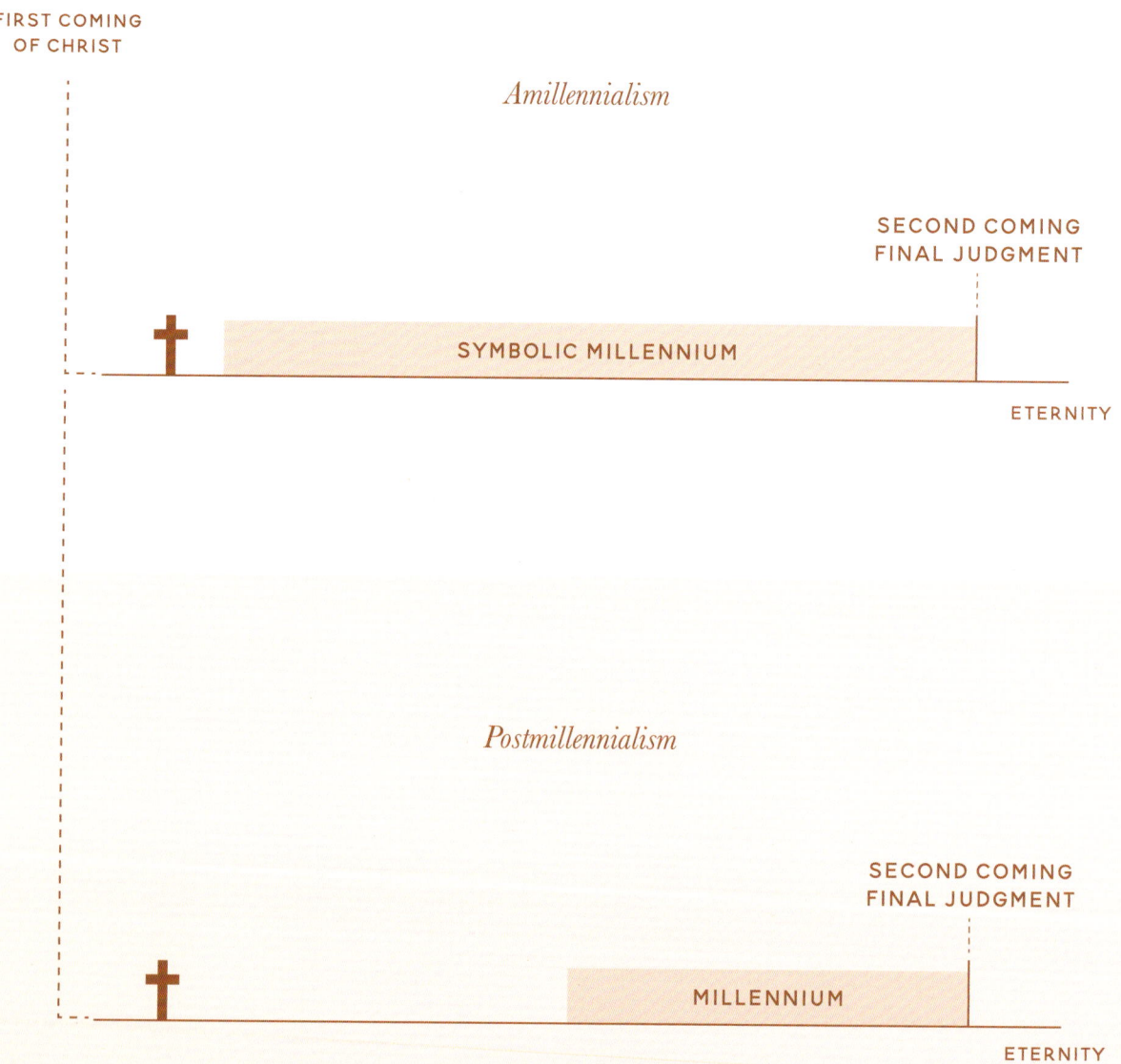

ESCHATOLOGY *Four Millennial Views*

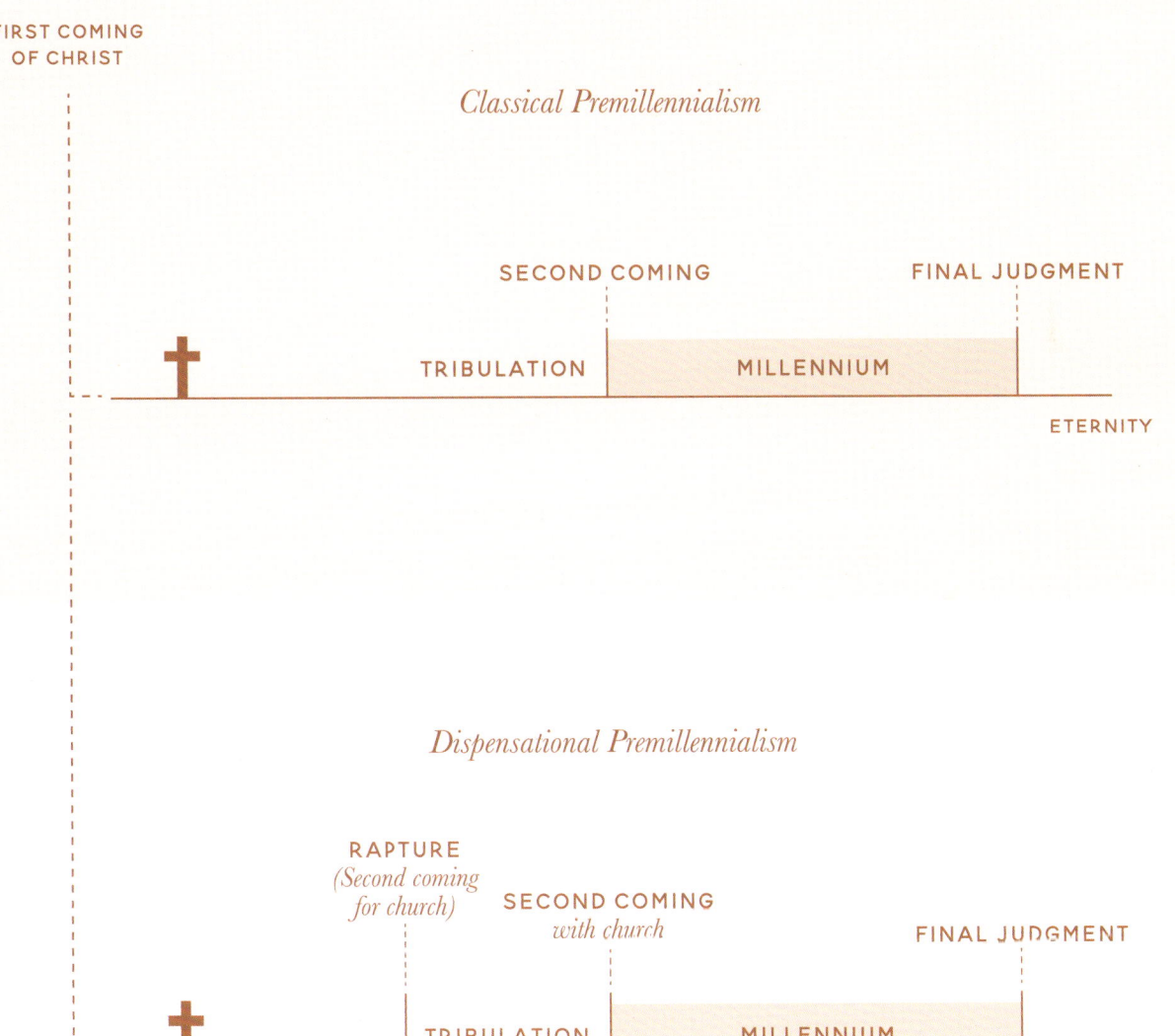

THE APPENDIX

TOPICAL REFERENCE OF CHARTS & ILLUSTRATIONS

TOPICAL REFERENCE OF CHARTS & ILLUSTRATIONS

Adoption	145	Condemnation	109
Angel of the Lord	71	Conversion	142
The Angel of the Lord in Scripture	70	*"Convert"*	142
Angels	188	Creation Mandate	101
"Angel"	189	*The Creation Mandate*	100
Ascension	129	Crucifixion	127
The Life of Christ Timeline	130	*The Life of Christ Timeline*	130
Attributes of God	24	Deity of Christ	117
Communicable and Incommunicable Attributes of God	24	Demons	191
		Actions of Demons	190
Baptism	174	Double Imputation	155
Baptism: A Display of Faith	175	*Double Imputation*	155
Two Views on Baptism	175	Election	139
Bible Translations	95	Eternal	26
Comparison of Bible Translations	94	*The Eternality of God*	26
Branches of Systematic Theology	17	Eternal Humanity of Christ	133
Calling	140	*Evidence of Christ's Bodily Resurrection*	*132*
General Call vs. Effectual Call	140	Eternality of Scripture	86
Canon	89	Faithful	28
The Canon of Scripture	88	*The Faithfulness of God*	29
Criteria for Canonization	90	Final Judgment	195
Church Government	182	*Are You Washed in the Blood?*	194
Models of Church Government	184	Fruit of the Spirit	163
Communion	177	*The Fruit of the Spirit*	162
Communion and the Passover	176	General Revelation	20
Differing Views of Communion	178		

APPENDIX

Glorification	149	Incarnation	115
Justification, Sanctification,		*"Immanuel"*	114
Glorification	149	Incomprehensible	65
Glorious	31	*The Knowledge of God*	64
Man's Highest Calling	30	Indwelling of the Holy Spirit	159
Good	32	*Indwelling of the Holy Spirit*	160
The Goodness of God	33	Inerrancy of Scripture	82
Gracious	35	*Discerning Truth from Error*	83
The Grace of God	34	Inspiration of Scripture	79
Heaven	200	*The Inspired Word of God*	80
Elements of Heaven	200	Jealous	41
Hell	201	*The Jealousy of God*	40
Elements of Hell	201	Just	42
Holy	36	*The Justice of God*	43
Response to God's Holiness	37	Justification	143
How to be Saved	136	Liturgy	181
The Metanarrative of Scripture	137	*"Liturgy"*	180
Humanity of Christ	118	Love	45
Hypostatic Union	119	*The Love of God*	44
Hypostatic Union	120	Merciful	46
Image of God	98	*The Mercy of God*	47
Imago Dei	99	Millennial Views	202
Immanent	67	*Millennial Views*	204
The Transcendence vs.		New Heaven and New Earth	196
Immanence of God	68	*Eden to Eternity*	197
Immutable	39	Offices of Christ	123
Our Unchanging God	39	*The Offices of Christ*	125

Omnipotent	49	Sovereign	62
The Power of God	48	*The Sovereignty of God*	62
Omnipresent	50	Special Revelation	21
The Omnipresence vs.		Spiritual Gifts	164
Manifest Presence of God	51	*Examples of Spiritual Gifts*	165
Omniscient	53	*Views of Miraculous Gifts*	166
Limited vs. Infinite Knowledge	52	Substitutionary Atonement	152
Ordinances and Sacraments	174	*Substitutionary Atonement*	153
Ordo Salutis	138	Sufficiency of Scripture	85
The Order of Salvation	138	*The Sufficiency of Scripture*	84
Original Languages of Scripture	92	Systematic Theology	13
Percentages of Original Languages	92	*Primary, Secondary, and*	
Examples of Original Languages	93	*Tertiary Issues*	14
Original Sin	106	True	57
Federal Headship	107	*Reflecting God's Truthfulness*	56
Patient	58	The Fall	105
The Fruit of Patience	59	*Effects of the Fall*	104
Perichoresis	22	Theophany	72
Perichoresis	23	*Theophanies in Scripture*	73
Perseverance	148	Total Depravity	110
Personhood of the Holy Spirit	158	*Effects of Total Depravity*	111
Roles of the Holy Spirit	160	Transcendent	66
Providence	75	*The Transcendence vs.*	
Regeneration	141	*Immanence of God*	68
Resurrection	128	Trinity	22
The Life of Christ Timeline	130	Types of Theology	10
Resurrection from the Dead	199	Union with Christ	151
Righteous	61	*Our Identity*	150
The Standard of Righteousness	60	Universal Church, Regional Church,	
Sanctification	146	and Local Church	170
Scale of Righteousness	147	*"Church"*	171

Virgin Birth	126
The Life of Christ Timeline	130
Visible and Invisible Church	173
The True Church	172
What is Sin?	102
Sin: A Matter of the Heart	103
What is Theology?	5
Why is Theology Important?	6
"Theology"	5
The Impacts of Theology	7
Types of Theology	8
Wise	54